Among Predators and Prey

Among
Predators
and Prey

Hugo van Lawick

Elm Tree Books

LONDON

First published in Great Britain 1986
by Elm Tree Books/Hamish Hamilton Ltd
Garden House, 57–59 Long Acre, London WC2E 9JZ

Copyright © 1986 by Hugo van Lawick

Design by Peter Campbell

Map by Patrick Leeson

British Library Cataloguing in Publication Data
Lawick, Hugo van
    Among predators and prey.
    1. Photography of animals   2. Predatory animals
    – Pictorial works
    I. Title
    779'.32'0924   TR729.P7
    ISBN 0-241-11792-5

Typeset by Rowland Phototypesetting Ltd
Bury St Edmunds, Suffolk
Printed and bound in Italy by
Arnoldo Mondadori Editore, Verona

TITLE: Thomson gazelles often frolic at sunset.

OVERLEAF (pp. 6–7): During the rainy season millions of animals migrate to the vast short grass plains of the Serengeti. Usually the Thomson gazelles arrive first because, with their small mouths, they are able to select the tender new grass shoots.

OVERLEAF (pp. 8–9): The wildebeest migration, consisting of about two million animals, moves away from the short grass plains when the dry season starts and roams through bush and acacia tree country where water is more readily available.

OVERLEAF (pp. 10–11): Lions sometimes prey on giraffes. By hitting or grabbing a giraffe's hindleg a lion can throw the large prey off balance and, once its victim is lying on the ground, has the opportunity to apply a bite to the throat.

Contents

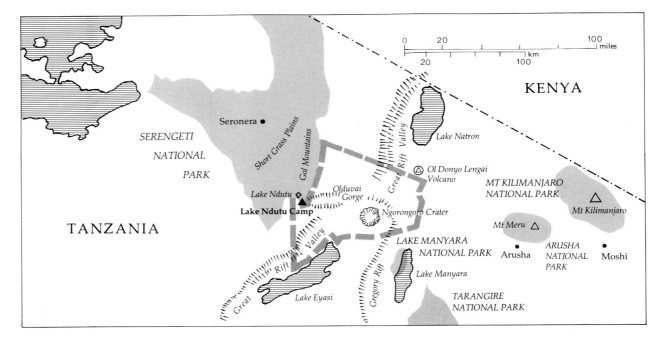

KENYA

SERENGETI NATIONAL PARK

Seronera •

Short Grass Plains

Gol Mountains

Great Rift Valley

Lake Natron

Ol Donyo Lengai Volcano

MT KILIMANJARO NATIONAL PARK

Mt Kilimanjaro △

Lake Ndutu

Olduvai Gorge

Lake Ndutu Camp

Ngorongoro Crater

Mt Meru △

TANZANIA

LAKE MANYARA NATIONAL PARK

• Arusha

ARUSHA NATIONAL PARK

• Moshi

Great Rift Valley

Gregory Rift

Lake Manyara

Great Rift Valley

Lake Eyasi

TARANGIRE NATIONAL PARK

0 20 100 miles
20 100 km

approximate boundaries
of National Parks and
Game Reserves

*(NGORONGORO CRATER)
CONSERVATION AREA*

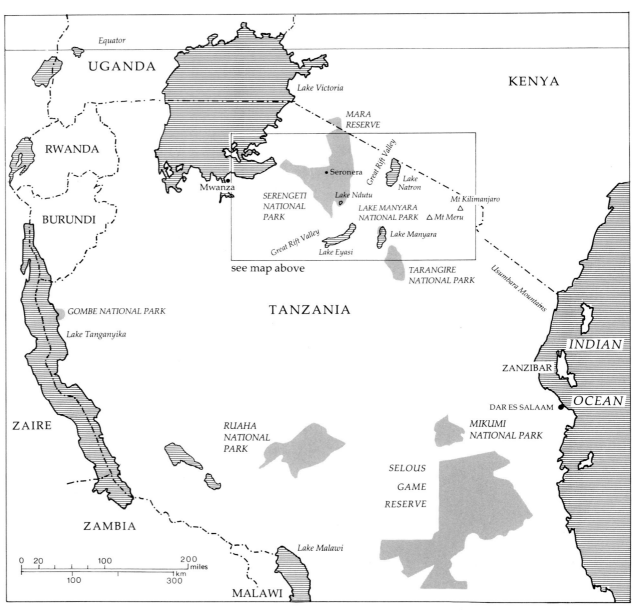

Equator

UGANDA

Lake Victoria

KENYA

RWANDA

MARA RESERVE

• Seronera

Great Rift Valley

Lake Natron

BURUNDI

Mwanza •

SERENGETI NATIONAL PARK

Lake Ndutu

LAKE MANYARA NATIONAL PARK

△ Mt Meru

Mt Kilimanjaro △

Great Rift Valley

Lake Eyasi

Lake Manyara

see map above

Usumbara Mountains

GOMBE NATIONAL PARK

Lake Tanganyika

TARANGIRE NATIONAL PARK

TANZANIA

INDIAN

ZAIRE

ZANZIBAR

DAR ES SALAAM •

OCEAN

RUAHA NATIONAL PARK

MIKUMI NATIONAL PARK

SELOUS GAME RESERVE

ZAMBIA

0 20 100 200 miles
100 300 km

Lake Malawi

MALAWI

Introduction

I have lived in tents among wild animals in Africa for twenty-five years. So most of my life. For six of those years I lived among wild chimpanzees in a forest on the shores of Lake Tanganyika and for seventeen years in the world's greatest wildlife area, the Serengeti, where I studied, filmed and photographed the behaviour of the large carnivores such as lions, leopards, cheetahs and wild dogs and their prey. For two years I filmed and photographed hyaenas and jackals in the giant Ngorongoro Crater and I spent six months in the Lake Manyara National Park where there are more elephants per square kilometre than anywhere else in Africa.

Life was a bit primitive when I started living in the wild. I had only one very small tent. This wasn't too bad during the dry season when I could sit at my campfire in the evenings, but during the rainy season, when tropical downpours flooded large areas, it was a constant battle to keep myself and more importantly my camera equipment dry and clean. So when I could afford it, I bought a larger tent with an enormous verandah. Subsequently, over the years, I slowly expanded my camping equipment further and life in the wild became quite comfortable. For many years I had a nomadic type of life style, only staying a few weeks or months in one spot before moving to another area. Then seventeen years ago I decided that I needed a permanent home as a base and so I erected ten tents in the shade of some acacia trees on the Serengeti. This base camp has been my home ever since.

I had wanted to be a wildlife film-maker and photographer since I was a teenager. At first I had visualised the excitement of travelling all over the world while doing this but I changed my mind soon after arriving in Africa from Holland. First of all I found the variety of scenery and animals in East Africa so extensive and fascinating that I had little urge to go elsewhere. In addition I decided that I would be able to do a far better job if I specialised in one or two areas and in the animals which live there. In this way I would get to know many of the animals as individuals and discover their distinct personalities. Establishing my home among the wild animals helped enormously.

In front of my home there is a beautiful view over a small blue lake, where thousands of pink flamingoes feed. To the left of the lake there is a small grass plain where wildebeest, zebras and gazelles graze and next to my camp impala and giraffes and pigmy antelopes browse from bushes and trees. All around my tents colourful sunbirds suck nectar from small flowers and weaver-birds and many others build their nests.

The lake in front of my camp and the area around it is called Ndutu, which

My son and I on our way to look for fossils. I never carry a fire arm but take along a Maasai spear on these expeditions (photo: Gerald Rilling)

in the Maasai language means 'a peaceful place'. Normally this is true. Recently, though, some lions tore their way into my bedroom tent and pulled the blankets off my bed. I was not in bed at the time. When I arrived some time later, I found the blankets scattered among the bushes and the lions lying in the branches of a nearby tree, looking absolutely innocent. Needless to say I slept in another tent that night. I also kept my only weapon, a Maasai spear, close at hand. More reassuringly I parked my landrover next to the tent.

When I woke at sunrise next morning, I peered out of the tent and found that the lions had moved to a small marsh below camp, where the four lionesses of the pride had sixteen small cubs. So I emerged from the tent. I had barely walked a metre before I was surrounded by numerous colourful birds which fluttered around my head, some almost landing on my shoulders. A little later, when I had breakfast, many of these birds landed on the table and I gave them a share of my food. Most of them were brilliantly coloured superb starlings but there was also a flock of rufous weavers, which nest in an acacia tree next to the camp, and numerous Swahili sparrows. At first I did not realise there was something under the table. Suddenly, however, I winced in pain: pecking at my big toe was a cheeky d'Arnaud's barbet, as if reminding me to give him something too. I gave him a piece of scrambled egg and watched him hop off to his nest, a hole in the ground nearby. Barbets are related to woodpeckers but luckily their beaks are not quite as sharp and forceful.

I have always wanted to live among animals. Where this interest came from, I do not know. Maybe it was from a very young age when my mother had a pet pigmy squirrel which continually wanted to make a nest in her hair. I presume that this little creature filled me with wonder. Later it found a mate in the garden but it regularly returned at tea time for a lump of sugar. This was in Indonesia, where I was born and where my father was an officer in the Dutch fleet air arm.

While my interest in animals may have started in Indonesia, it was fostered in Devon where we moved after my father was killed in a plane crash when I was four. We lived in a tiny village, called Stoodleigh, at the edge of extensive woods. Here I spent much of my time, when not at the local school, Ravenswood, with a friend of mine, Peter Byles, playing in the woods and watching animals and fairly ignorant, I guess, about the war. In fact I was not helpful to the war effort because I saved a lot of rabbits by setting off the traps and snares.

I realised recently that my interest in outdoor life must have been intense even at the age of seven, because I revisited Stoodleigh for the first time forty years later, and recognised most of the country, even individual trees. However, I was completely taken by surprise by the large and splendid interior of Ravenswood School. It had obviously made no impression on me whatsoever as a youngster.

After the war, when I was ten, we moved to Holland. While I had enjoyed school in England, I hated it in Holland where there was a greater emphasis on cramming facts and sports, which I loved and was good at, were considered less important. I soon started longing for the time when I would be old enough to leave school and began wondering what I could do in order to live in the wild, preferably among lots of animals.

The revelation came to me when I was fifteen years old. I was on a three-day trip with ten friends in Holland to a national park north of Arnhem. One of my friends had a 8mm camera with a standard lens and we had decided to make a short film about the trip, sharing the costs. Filming the shy deer and wild Mouflon sheep proved to be a problem, for they looked like specks in the viewfinder. Obviously we had to get closer and I was chosen for the job since I was the best in the group at creeping up on animals. The difficulty was that I had no idea what the strange figures on the side of the lens meant and there was no time to teach me. So whenever we saw an animal in the distance, my

ABOVE LEFT: Giraffes frequently wander through my camp as do lions and many other creatures.

ABOVE RIGHT: The elephants soon got so used to me that I could be among them and photograph details of their behaviour otherwise difficult to capture (photo: Ferry Kleemann).

OVERLEAF: Lions in the Lake Manyara National Park often rest in trees. There are probably various reasons for this behaviour, less frequently seen in other areas: avoiding a species of biting fly, coolness, spotting prey and avoiding elephants with which they have an antagonistic relationship.

friends enquired how close I thought I could get to it and then preset the distance and diaphragm before I set off. I was very successful in my first attempts and got lots of film material of the animals: all looking briefly in amazement and then turning their rumps to the camera and running off. Not really what we wanted nor very nice for the animals. However I now knew what I wanted to do as a job.

On completing my schooling and national service in the Dutch army, I joined a film company in Amsterdam as an assistant cameraman. This company made commercials and I learned a lot about how to operate a camera. But I now know that I should have included a period as an assistant editor before starting film-making myself, because it is in the editing room that one learns what shots a cameraman needs to take to make a good film. Some of the most valuable information on story construction I did not learn from professionals but from two amateurs. As an assistant cameraman I was only allowed to clean and load cameras and put them on a tripod, and I was longing to be able to operate a camera. So I got together with two amateurs who wanted to make a film. For four or five months we met one evening a week in order to write a script. The story was a simple one about four boys on a holiday. Most of our time during the script-writing was spent in discussing the totally different personalities of each of the four main characters, determining what they would do and how they would react in different circumstances. Unfortunately the film was never made but the knowledge I obtained of the importance of personality was invaluable. I was already sure that, like humans, each animal also had its own personality and this was the aspect of wildlife film-making which I wanted to cover. As it turned out, it would be another ten years before I could accomplish this. Before then I had to work as a cameraman for other people, making documentaries which concentrated on the general behaviour of animals. I tried repeatedly to persuade my employers to let me make a film on individual animals as personalities but was unsuccessful. It had never been done before with wild animals.

Having completed a two-year apprenticeship in Holland as an assistant cameraman, I departed for East Africa where I started work as a cameraman, filming for Armand and Michaela Denis on their TV series 'On Safari', famous at the time. I was twenty-two and it was tremendously exciting to be in Africa at last and to start filming animals.

During the next two years I filmed creatures ranging in size from insects to elephants and camped in a number of wildlife areas in Kenya and Uganda. To my frustration, however, much of the filming was on captive animals, an aspect of wildlife photography which I hate for many reasons, mainly because it often involves using animals in what I consider to be immoral ways. Often the photographer is concerned only with photographic results and has little regard for the animal's feelings or even at times its survival. One famous series of wildlife pictures showed a leopard catching and killing a baboon. A tame leopard had been used and fifteen or so captive baboons in turn had been released in front of the leopard and killed before the photographer was satisfied he had some spectacular pictures. He was given the 'Photographer of the Year' award. Luckily Armand and Michaela Denis did not expect me to do this sort of thing, nor would I have agreed to it, but all the same I did not like working with their captive animals.

One way I got round this was by filming insects and this had a major effect on my photography. I used light reflectors such as mirrors, to create and experiment with lighting effects. This is the essence of photography. Amateur photographers are usually advised to keep the sun behind them but strict adherence to this method produces flat photographs with no feeling of depth. It is the 'safest' type of photography because it is the easiest with which to ascertain the correct aperture and some experience is needed to determine how much contrast each type of film can take. Usually, when the light is not too harsh, I try to photograph more or less against the light and even when the light is harsh, I rarely keep the sun directly behind me; I prefer it to be ten degrees or so to the side, so that the hairs on an animal cast a slight shadow and thus create more depth and contrast.

On completion of two years' work for the Denis's, and at the age of twenty-four, I was fortunate to be able to work for the National Geographic Society as their photographer in East Africa. From then on I was almost continually in the wild, mainly filming and photographing animals, but also being involved in the work of Drs Louis and Mary Leakey as they excavated the fossil remains of prehistoric man in the Olduvai Gorge and elsewhere. The most difficult assignment the National Geographic Society gave me was to film the studies on wild chimpanzee behaviour by Jane Goodall. Originally this was only going to be a seven-week project during which I was to film how Jane lived in the forest but was not expected to get much on the chimpanzees, since it was realised how difficult this would be. As it turned out I did manage to get much more film on the chimpanzees than anticipated, including a chimpanzee making and using twig tools to capture termites. This was the most important discovery Jane had made on the chimpanzees at that stage.

The film material on the chimpanzees was intended for a lecture film which Jane would narrate. Having been successful in filming the chimpanzees, however, I could visualise that with additional filming we could make a TV film. As it turned out the National Geographic was planning to start producing television films for the first time and so it was agreed that I should return to the chimpanzees for nine months of further filming on Jane and the chimpanzees. At the end of that period a number of important events took place. Jane and I got married early in 1964 and I started planning to film the chimpanzees over many years, maybe as much as a decade, so that we would end up with more or less a life story of some of the individuals. As it turned out it was to

OVERLEAF: Olive baboons are one of the most adaptable primate species, inhabiting a large variety of habitats, including open country and forests.

OPPOSITE TOP: A white or square lipped rhino, followed by an egret catching insects disturbed by the rhino, rubs itself on a termite mound. Within East Africa this species only occurred in Uganda where it has been exterminated since this picture was taken in 1966.

OPPOSITE BOTTOM: Warthogs are often prey to the larger predators but, with their large tusks, are sometimes successfully able to confront a predator.

cover twenty-three years, during which I spent six years with the chimpanzees in the forest and three years editing the film.

Although I spent the whole of 1964 with Jane among the chimpanzees, I also had other photographic work to do. From 1965 onwards, Jane and I spent part of each year with the chimpanzees and the rest on the Serengeti or in the Ngorongoro Crater. In order that Jane's scientific research on the chimpanzees would have no gaps, we took on assistants and subsequently up to 15 scientists to continue the work in the forest and were able to speak daily to them by radio. Usually while I photographed or filmed the animals of the Serengeti, Jane worked in camp in her travelling office, a VW bus, analysing her notes on chimpanzee behaviour. However in 1966 we decided to write a book on the wild dogs, hyaenas and jackals. To do this we would have to study these animals first and as I would be unable to cover all three species, it was decided that she would research and write the chapter on hyaenas. To study the hyaenas and jackals we lived for a year in the Ngorongoro Crater. By then Jane was pregnant but insisted that she would be all right staying in the wild until three weeks before the birth of our child. In fact, if Jane had been of a nervous disposition, our son Hugo would almost certainly have been born, a little prematurely, among roaring lions in the Ngorongoro Crater. In fact the three African assistants we had with us at the time maintained our son should have been named Simba (Lion) as a result.

We were camping along the Munge River in the Ngorongoro Crater and planned to go to Nairobi a few days later in expectation of the birth. Quite regularly in the evenings one or more of the local lions lay within fifty metres of our tents and occasionally roared. This did not worry us particularly: they never appeared to take much notice of the camp and there was plenty of natural prey around. In the evenings, Jane and I usually sat in our dining/office tent transcribing our day's notes. One long side of the tent was always rolled up so that we could see the moon and the stars and could hear the sounds of the animals, although the softer sounds were obscured a bit by the noise of a pressure lamp by which we worked. Looking out in the night, or even at dusk, we could not see much because our eyes had adjusted to the bright light of the lamp. Just after dusk one evening, I heard one of our assistants call from a tent some distance away. Unable to hear him clearly, I wandered out of the tent and heard him warn me urgently that there was a lion in camp. By now my eyes had started to adjust to the darkness and I noticed two lions not far away, creeping up on me. I called Jane and she joined me but we had barely taken a step towards the landrover, parked five metres away, when a third lion appeared from behind the vehicle. We retreated into the tent and hastily closed the flap.

Once this was done, I grabbed a panga – a large knife and the only weapon around – and then lit a gas stove and put a lot of paper next to it, ready to use fire in order to try and drive off any lion that tried to enter. Unfortunately there were no windows in the tent and so all we could do was listen to sounds. To

my amazement loud music suddenly blared from the kitchen tent. Then we heard a scream, followed by pots and pans clattering about wildly, and the radio went dead. Obviously one or more of our assistants were in trouble and with the lions over by the kitchen tent we could probably make it to the car and rush to their aid. In a split second decision I unzipped our tent, but hastily zipped it closed again when I found a lion right next to it. I called out to our assistants, enquiring whether they were all right, but got no answer. There was deathly silence. Then I heard a tent being ripped. Then more silence while I racked my brains to think of a way in which Jane, heavily pregnant, and I could escape.

Obviously the lions had killed our assistants. Suddenly, I heard human feet running fast toward the car: two of our assistants were still alive and trying to escape. To my amazement I heard three car doors slam: they had all escaped. Soon afterwards, they called to us that the lions were far enough away for us to make it to the landrover too. Once inside the landrover we could see the three lions playing next to the kitchen tent. Apparently all three assistants had been inside this tent when the lions entered the camp. They had switched on the radio thinking the loud noise would frighten the lions off, but the opposite had happened: one of the lions had been attracted by it and had poked its large shaggy head into the tent. The assistants had thrown pots and pans at it and the lion retreated. From then on our assistants had decided any sound was a bad idea and had therefore wisely ignored my calls. They had, however, been able to peer out and had seen one of the lions rip its way into a neighbouring bedroom tent and flop on to a bed for a while, before emerging and starting to play with the other two.

It took us half an hour to chase the lions out of the camp with the car. They didn't want to go, for they were in a playful mood and seemed to think that at last we had agreed to join in the game! These lions were sub-adults and I have subsequently discovered that they are the ones to look out for when camping, because they are often inquisitive and playful.

Anyway, it was a narrow escape, and a few days later we left for Nairobi where Jane gave birth to our son, Hugo. About a month later we took him to live in the forest, 1500 kilometres from Nairobi, where we had been studying and filming chimpanzees.

Raising a small child among wild animals involved taking numerous safeguards, for I have seen only too often that predators, including chimpanzees, are attracted to young creatures: but in order to eat them, not because they want to adopt them as the apes did in the story of Tarzan. To safeguard Hugo as a baby, Jane and I erected a small prefabricated house with barred windows in the forest. However, adult male chimpanzees are three to four times stronger than a man and so in case a chimpanzee managed to force its way into the building, we kept Hugo in his cot in a large cage within the house. In fact the first time the chimpanzees heard tiny Hugo crying, they rushed to the windows

OPPOSITE TOP: When a lioness is in oestrus she is mated about every fifteen minutes over a period of ten days. She and the male commonly snarl at each other during the climax of mating.

OPPOSITE BOTTOM: A male baboon's canine teeth are as long as those of a leopard and make it a formidable adversary. During encounters I have seen between baboons and leopards, the large cats always retreated.

of the house and stared in with their hair out, a threatening sign, and expressions on their faces which I had seen when they hunt monkeys, baboons, bushbuck and bush pigs. Of course when Hugo started to crawl we couldn't confine him to a cage and we erected a new simple house on the edge of the forest and on the beach of Lake Tanganyika. The chimpanzees only rarely go there, but large troops of baboons forage there frequently. Although they do not eat human babies, as chimpanzees have been known to do, they can be aggressive and the powerful males with teeth as long as those of a leopard are to be feared. This meant that Hugo had to be watched every second of the day, either by Jane or myself or, when we were working, by an African 'bodyguard'.

However, he survived, and lived in the wild until he was nine years old, at times among the chimpanzees and at other times on the Serengeti plains. After Jane and I went our separate ways, they also spent a lot of time on the coast near Dar es Salaam.

Working as a photographer or film cameraman usually means that one is part of a team. A wildlife photographer may do the photography alone but usually others are responsible for deciding how the material is edited. Even though the editors may be the best in the world, the end result is nearly always different from what the photographer had in mind. There is an advantage in this system, for a photographer may be too close to his work and this can make it difficult for him to make dispassionate editing decisions. All the same I found it frustrating not to be involved fully in the editing decisions on my own material and so, after seven years' experience in East Africa, I decided to become an independent producer/director in addition to a photographer. Throughout the next eighteen years I produced my own films and photographs.

Filming animals requires a great deal of time and patience and so the more time I could spend among them the better. This, in addition to my boyhood wish to live in the wild, gave me plenty of excuse to establish my tented home on the Serengeti rather than have a house in a town in East Africa as a base. This was only possible because over the years I had helped the conservation causes of the area in a number of ways and as a result and much to my surprise and delight was designated an honorary resident for the rest of my life. This is a highly unusual honour which has never been bestowed on anyone else, except that the resident Maasai are allowed by birthright to live in the 'conservation area' part of the Serengeti.

My tented home, the base camp at Ndutu, is quite comfortable, each tent being the equivalent of a room in a house. Thus, apart from my bedroom tent, I have two guest tents, a dining tent, an office tent and even a sitting room tent which contains a fairly extensive library. I used to have a kitchen tent but the local hyaenas pushed their way into it and stole my supper so often that I replaced it with a small corrugated iron building to which I attached a large store for my considerable supplies of food, vehicle spares and so on. I always buy enough supplies to last for many months, because the closest town is three hundred kilometres away and two hundred kilometres of that is a rough dirt road. To make the building as unobtrusive as possible, I camouflaged it by painting it green and superimposing the shapes of trees in a darker colour. Next to the kitchen are two 4500 litre tanks in which I store rain water, enough to last through the six month dry season and even a year or so of drought. If I run out of water, the closest natural resource is ninety kilometres away on the rim of Ngorongoro Crater.

Lots of animals live in my camp or visit it regularly. Numerous antelopes and gazelles such as graceful impala, Thomson and Grant's gazelles and tiny dikdiks, pigmy antelopes, graze on the lawn in front of the tents and giraffes often browse from the acacia trees surrounding the camp or even the ones providing shade for the tents. Quite often, too, a small herd of elephants feeds from nearby trees, uprooting some of them; recently they came right into camp and started demolishing my favourite tree which shades the sitting room tent. I objected strongly, screaming loudly and luckily the elephants moved slightly and pushed over a tree at the edge of camp.

One of my favourite animals is a slender-bodied genet cat which lives in the store at daytime and roams about the camp at night. She has become so used to me that she will enter the dining tent for a share of my supper and sometimes I see her silhouetted in the moonlight as she hunts among the branches above my tents. On a few occasions when I scratched on the bark of the tree below, she crept down and tapped gently at my fingers, playing with them.

In the evenings, after supper, I often like to sit in the dark outside my tents and listen to the sounds of the African night. Having lived in the wild for so many years I have got to know many of the sounds well and am able to tell what is happening even though I cannot see the events. On one such evening recently, I was sitting at a log fire outside my dining tent and I could hear the tearing of grass. From the sound I knew it was zebras grazing and not wildebeest. Then a hyaena giggled hysterically. It was being chased; most likely it had a scrap of food and was being pursued by another hyaena, intent on a share. Soon afterwards a family of golden jackals howled, two adults and four cubs, and this turned into excited yapping: the adults and cubs were greeting each other. A little later a lion roared loudly. This did not worry me: at least I knew where he was, about 500 metres away. But suddenly I tensed and listened carefully: two silver-back jackals were yapping nearby. Their alarm calls were continuous and they were moving along the edge of camp. Then I relaxed: they were moving away . . . 50 metres . . . 100 metres . . . 200 metres. I knew they were following a leopard, warning their cubs and everyone else of its whereabouts and I could imagine the annoyed flicking of the leopard's tail, its hunting efforts frustrated.

A little later an almost full moon appeared on the horizon. As the moon rose, the surrounding countryside slowly became visible and I could see the

OVERLEAF: Up to half a million or so flamingoes often reside in a small lake in the giant Ngorongoro Crater where they are preyed upon by fish eagles, jackals, serval cats, and spotted hyaenas.

27

OPPOSITE TOP: Young spotted hyaenas, in this case the offspring of two females, often rest at the entrance of a communal den. Unable to compete for solid food with the adults, hyaena cubs are dependent on their mother's milk for about eighteen months.

OPPOSITE BOTTOM: Bat-eared foxes prey on insects and are able to hear beetle larvae feeding underground.

dark shapes of wildebeests grazing. Although I had clearly heard zebras grazing nearby earlier, they were almost invisible, their black and white stripes effectively breaking up their shapes so that they were camouflaged in the moonlight. But being invisible, even completely invisible, does not give complete protection from predators. I saw a bat-eared fox, a small creature with large ears, apparently listening carefully to the ground. It obviously heard something for it suddenly started digging and soon afterwards it was eating something, probably a beetle grub.

Much of my photographic work takes me far from the camp at Ndutu, sometimes for many months. This is particularly true when I revisit the chimpanzees, a journey of twelve hundred kilometres. Even within the Serengeti, however, I often live for long periods away from Ndutu. This is not really surprising, for the Serengeti is equal in size to the Netherlands, Belgium and Luxembourg put together and when following an animal in order to film its life, I must be able to be with it from dawn to dusk and sometimes through the night also.

Depending on how far I am going from my base camp and for how long, I can organise myself in different ways. On short trips of only a few days, I can sleep in my landrover which has been especially equipped for this purpose. On trips lasting for a week or so, I can take some lightweight tents and for longer trips lasting a month or more, a complete, self-contained camp.

To help me with my work and looking after the base camp, I am assisted by five Tanzanians, Sirili, Lawrence, Renatus, Maro and Daniel. Living in isolation among wild animals as we do, we are, of course, dependent on each other for safety and our relationships are very much as one might find in a family.

Sirili is in charge. He was in the medical corps in Burma during the Second World War and subsequently worked for the film star, Hardy Kruger, who lived in Tanzania for a while. Renatus and Lawrence are mechanics, able to repair anything from cars to generators. These three often accompany me on safaris while Maro, who has lived in the wild all his life, and Paulo, who is a carpenter, take care of the tented home at Ndutu.

During the eighteen years I have worked independently in the wild, I have alternated between making films and taking still photographs. The main reason for this is that it can be both difficult and frustrating finding the necessary financial support for the type of films which I want to make. I also enjoy still photography which, at times, is a relief from film-making. This is because producing (or 'making') a film is a full-time job, lasting from dawn until late at night. In addition to the actual filming and cleaning of cameras and so on, one has to think constantly about what has been filmed and what else is needed to make a sequence work. For instance one may have filmed a lioness jumping on to a zebra and bringing it down. This, on its own, will not be sufficient for a good dramatic film. To make it work properly one needs material of a lioness stalking and shots of zebras not noticing the lioness getting closer. Not only

this but the shots must be obtained in the same or similar surroundings to the successful kill, say in dry grass, and the lighting conditions must also correspond, say hazy sunlight. This is an obvious example but the same applies to less dramatic events. Still photography is quite different. In general individual pictures stand on their own and it is less vital or not important at all to make them part of a tight-fitting sequence.

Many wildlife photographers make extensive use of hides. This is necessary with shy species, but I try to avoid using hides because I want to be able to follow my subjects in order to get different angles and as much intimate detail of their daily lives as possible. This means either that I have to choose individual animals which are not frightened of a car or that I have to habituate the animals to my presence, by first observing them from a distance and then gradually moving closer over a period of days, weeks or even months. Nearly all the animals I have worked with ultimately accepted me to such an extent that I could be within a few metres without them taking the slightest notice, even when I drove along parallel to them as they wandered around. Originally I thought it would be possible to habituate any animal to this extent, but this is not necessarily correct. I remember studying a pair of golden jackals in the Ngorongoro Crater. The female gave birth to four cubs and although her mate and cubs sometimes lay in the shade of my car, she never accepted me completely. Perhaps she had had a bad experience with a car when she was young.

In many East African national parks it is possible to get quite close to a lot of the animals without disturbing them, making it possible to watch their behaviour in detail. A few tourists complain that it is not right for the animals to be so accustomed to man, that the parks are more like large zoos and that areas where the animals are shy are much more natural. In fact the opposite is true. Before man invented bows and arrows and fire arms he would have wandered fairly closely among the animals and could probably play with some of them: chimpanzees and baboons quite often have friendly games even though chimpanzees sometimes hunt baboons. Even the carnivores are able to wander among their prey when not hunting.

Extreme fear of man is therefore a recent development, and the distances animals flee have increased as weapons become deadly at greater and greater distances. Creeping up on a shy animal undoubtedly satisfies some primitive hunting instinct, but I much prefer to watch undisturbed animals; it gives one a greater understanding of their natural behaviour and the personality of individuals.

I have always been most interested in animals as individuals. Each has its own distinct character and I have tried to reflect this in my films as much as possible. For instance when I started filming wild chimpanzees, there was one adolescent male, Figan, about nine years old, who was exceptionally brainy for a chimpanzee and also absolutely determined to become dominant over the

OPPOSITE TOP:
Appearing to be giving itself a dust bath, I suspected this elephant was in fact threatening me by repeatedly throwing a clump of grass into the air.

OPPOSITE BOTTOM: Baboons do not shelter from the rain, except maybe occasionally among rocks. In the forest there would be little opportunity to do so since heavy tropical downpours penetrate even the thickest vegetation.

33

Two orphan wildebeest calves narrowly escape three lionesses. Orphan wildebeest calves are common, having often been separated from their mother because of a low flying plane or a car driving too fast through the migration.

Two spotted hyaenas cross a flooded valley after heavy rain. Spotted hyaenas sometimes hide excess food under water where it is out of sight and reach of most other predators.

OVERLEAF: Buffalo sometimes find protection from lions by congregating in large herds. Even so, the lions in the Lake Manyara National Park live almost exclusively on buffalo.

others of his own age group. But he did not manage to dominate his twelve-year-old brother, Faben, until Faben contracted polio which paralysed one arm permanently. Figan immediately attacked his disabled brother and so established his dominance over him. As is often the case in humans, young brothers squabble but as they become older, they become closer to one another and this happened with Figan and Faben. Figan then cleverly used his brother in order to become dominant over the other chimpanzees in his community: he sought confrontations with others when his brother, Faben, was there to give him moral support, but studiously avoided any conflict when Faben was not there. This strategy paid off and Figan became the top-ranking male of the community.

Of course chimpanzees are very similar to man in many ways, but individuals have their own distinct character among other species too. I remember watching a family of golden jackals and noting that one of the cubs was far more inquisitive than his siblings. When this cub saw his parents eating mushrooms, he immediately tried one too. However he had not watched carefully enough, for he ate a mushroom of a different species and this apparently gave him hallucinations: he ran around in circles and subsequently he charged a Thomson gazelle and a wildebeest, both of which stared in apparent amazement at the tiny golden ball of fur and fled. Luckily the cub survived his experience.

One of the great animal characters I met was a warthog. This happened purely by chance. I had been following and photographing a female leopard and her two-year-old male cub, as large as his mother, for four months. The mother leopard had left to hunt but I decided to stay with the cub, who appeared to be in a frisky mood. He moved along a branch of a *Kigelia* tree which bore numerous large sausage-shaped fruits and brushed against one of the fruits. The fruit swayed away but on its return bumped into the leopard's bottom.

The leopard swung around, growled at the fruit and hit it with one of his paws. This then turned into a game, the leopard patting at various fruits so that finally the whole lot of them were swinging back and forth. When the leopard tired of this game, he descended the tree and pounced on the end of a dead branch. The other end of the branch bounced up towards the leopard, but he jumped aside and attacked it again, pinning it to the ground. When the branch stopped moving, the leopard continued on his way, occasionally patting at bits of vegetation. He had not gone far, however, when he spotted a warthog grazing peacefully. The leopard froze, flexed his legs until his tummy touched the grass and then crept forward. The warthog had its back to the predator and the leopard had no trouble getting close enough to pounce right on to the warthog's back. The warthog gave a tremendous snort of surprise and then pirouetted frantically, trying to throw the leopard off. I felt sure it was going to be killed but then, to my amazement, the leopard nimbly jumped off the pig's back and bounded playfully after a butterfly. Equally surprising was that the warthog merely watched the leopard go and then calmly continued to graze as if nothing had happened.

I met this warthog again a year later. I was watching a pack of wild dogs resting in the shade of a tree in the same area when the warthog appeared, walked straight up to the dogs and lay down among them. I was flabbergasted: warthogs are favourite food to wild dogs and sure enough the large pack immediately jumped up and surrounded the pig. The warthog got up and faced them calmly. The dogs hesitated, for the warthog had large tusks and dogs normally do not risk attacking a large prey unless it is running away, when they can attack from the rear. However, the warthog refused to run and merely spun around if a dog approached its rear. Finally the dogs gave up and lay down again. The warthog joined them and they all rested peacefully together.

The excitement of photography is that one is learning all the time, not only about the subjects being photographed but also about photography itself. I started off as an 'artistic' photographer: by this I mean I was mainly interested in lighting effects and composition. I then became more concerned with trying to obtain action pictures of animals and subsequently I tried to combine the two. My great weakness was that I was concentrating so much on details of animal behaviour that my pictures rarely included landscapes and in fact I did not know how to take good scenic pictures. I decided to train myself in this aspect, especially as I was trying to get a feature film off the ground in which landscapes would be vitally important. To do this I spent a year taking still photographs of animals in landscapes, experimenting with different lighting effects and focal length lenses. Most of all I looked and looked again at landscapes, and tried to soak up the feeling of each landscape in different seasons and at different times of day. It was a wonderfully rewarding experience which made me appreciate even more the great variety of landscapes in East Africa.

The short grass plains near the Gol Mountains are one of my favourite areas on the Serengeti. The Serengeti's name means 'a large place' and this is well illustrated on the short grass plains: they stretch as far as the horizon and one can gaze out and see no sign of any manmade thing, let alone another human being. In the dry season this area is almost a desert and only creatures which can manage for long periods without water can survive there. Most of the country is slightly undulating, reminding one of a gently rolling sea, and here and there small rock islands, called kopjes, offer shade and refuge for a variety of creatures, ranging from small rodents to lions. During the heavy rains, however, the area is transformed into a lush green carpet of tender grass and colourful flowers. Millions of animals migrate here from hundreds of kilometres away and the landscape is transformed.

I remember recently sitting on a rock overlooking this landscape. Colourful agama lizards, the males bright blue and orange, the females dull brown and camouflaged, scurried up and down its sides or hid in crevices at the slightest danger. Danger was everywhere. There was a very large and deadly puff adder curled up and motionless at the base of the rock and a lizard buzzard which,

OPPOSITE: Elephant calves love chasing birds. However, many birds have become so used to this behaviour that they totally ignore the little elephant's threats. This almost invariably unnerves the calf which is likely to run back to its mother and hide between her legs.

as its name implies, specialises in hunting lizards, including agama lizards, was perched in a nearby acacia tree.

On another rock, about a hundred metres from the one I was sitting on, there was a small pride of lions, a black-maned male with four females. They were waiting for the sun to set, as were the hyaenas lying in the cool mud of a nearby waterhole. In the opposite direction, about fifty metres away, there was a group of dens in which a pack of wild dogs rested and behind me, in the Gol Mountains, I knew a leopard also waited for the coolness of night.

For as far as the eye could see, which was a long way, at least fifty or sixty kilometres in most directions, the plains were covered by animals. I could probably see half a million wildebeest or more and quarter of a million or so gazelles. To my left, coming along a small valley, there was a herd of thirty elands and on the brow of a small hill a number of giraffes browsed from acacia trees.

In this landscape which had been my home for much of my life there was a great feeling of peace. It was not in the least apparent that all of us were alert as we sought to avoid being killed and eaten. Looking, listening, smelling, ready to run or hide. Even the vegetation tried to escape, the acacia trees defending themselves with thorns and the sodom apples with poison. Yet as each prey had developed a protective system, so some predator or other had usually found a way to deal with it.

The interrelationships between predators and prey had always fascinated me. Initially I considered only the meat-eaters as predators. Then I realised that in a way every animal is both a predator and a prey. For instance, the giraffe can be said to be a predator of acacia trees. During my photographic work I had mainly concentrated on the meat-eaters, the carnivores, but while watching them hunt, I could not help but notice the varied systems the prey used in order to escape their predators. I began to wonder how these systems had developed in evolution, especially with regard to mammals. Of course the behaviour of animals is not fossilised. Much is, however, inherited and gives us clues as to how the ancestors of today's animals behaved. To understand the development of the predators' and prey's behaviour better, I would have to think back to the time when life started in the sea and then follow the animals' development as they invaded the land, lived in forests and finally emerged on to the open plains.

1. The Beginning

I had the opportunity of considering how the relationship between predators and prey had developed when I went to visit my son who was staying with his mother on the tropical beach near Dar es Salaam where she lives when she is not in the forest studying chimpanzees. I had driven the 1500 kilometres from my camp to Dar es Salaam to collect a new landrover I had ordered from England. Renatus had been with me, but as we had a few days to spare he had gone to visit some friends.

Jane's house looks out over a beach of pure white sand with the blue sea thirty metres beyond. Living here and swimming among the coral reefs has fostered Hugo's interest in fish, which started on the beaches of Lake Tanganyika, where he spent a lot of time as a child. The water of the lake is so clear that one can see ten metres down and admire the numerous colourful fish.

I don't know much about fish, having spent little time on the coast, and so Hugo arranged for us to go out in a boat next day and explore the few small islands and coral reefs lying just off shore. As we waded through the small clear pools on the island, I continually stopped in amazement to look at the enormous variety of strange and colourful creatures which swam or crawled among the coral or weeds.

I reached down to pick up a colourful shell but Hugo, who had been keeping an eye on me, said, 'Watch out! Hold that shell by its side. It's got a poisonous barb which it can shoot out of the rear.'

I gingerly put it back in the pool and we continued on our way, but we hadn't gone far before my son warned me of a new danger:

'Look out! Lots of sea urchins among the weeds here. Don't step on them. It's almost impossible to get their spines out of your feet. Very painful too. Oh, look! Isn't that fish beautiful? Don't go too near it, though, it's a scorpion fish. Very poisonous. Quick, look at that one there – it can give you an electric shock. By the way, watch out for camouflaged stone fish. There are lots here. Their poison is so painful you will drown in a few centimetres of water.'

I started to tiptoe. It seemed a highly dangerous place to me – far more dangerous than living among lions.

On reaching a large pool we sat down and remained motionless, hoping to see some of the creatures interact with each other. I could see a large starfish wrap itself around a shell and, once its thousands of little suction feet had

OPPOSITE TOP: In prehistoric times, before the continents drifted apart, East Africa did not border the sea. Now it contains beautiful beaches fringed by palm trees. It also used to have an extensive coral reef but most of this has been destroyed by the daily use of dynamite for fishing.

OPPOSITE BOTTOM: A living example of how the first fishes may have evolved to live out of water, mudskippers often chase insects across land and cling for long periods on to the aboreal roots of mangroves.

attached themselves to both sides of the shell, it forcefully pulled it open, feeding on the contents. I knew that one shell owner, the queen scallop, depicted on the Shell petrol signs, can escape starfish by bounding away in fast leaps. One doesn't expect shells to jump but the queen scallop accomplishes this by flapping its shells quickly and thereby producing a sort of jet propulsion. The systems used by sea creatures to escape their predators are extremely varied and often remarkable. I cannot imagine, for instance, which predator would attempt to eat a box fish. It is completely enclosed in a thick external armoury, a crate of bones, with only its fins sticking out. I can imagine something trying to eat a small puffer fish, but would love to see the predator's reaction when the small fish suddenly becomes a big fish. The puffer fish accomplishes this by rapidly gulping air into its stomach.

In the pool I could see a number of sea cucumbers. They are not very attractive-looking creatures, although some predators may think they are rather tasty. However, the sea cucumber, when bothered by a predator, quickly extrudes its internal organs, leaving the attacker covered in a sticky mess. If the attacker has taken a bite from the sticky mess, the sea cucumber grows another set of entrails. We did not see anything try to attack one of the sea cucumbers but we did see a medium-sized fish suddenly dash forward and catch a smaller fish. While it was eating it, a horrifying, snake-like head with staring eyes emerged from a dark cave. Opening its mouth, which contained a long row of sharp teeth, the moray eel shot forward and quickly swallowed the medium-sized fish and its prey.

While my son and I sat at the edge of the sea, I considered the fact that it was here in the sea that life had begun, where the predators and prey had been born. What had there been before that? How and why had it all started?

Richard Dawkins' book, *The Selfish Gene*, contains a fascinating theory. In effect it says that predators and prey existed before life began. Furthermore that the competition between these proto-predators and prey was what caused life to evolve.

When the earth was born, it was populated by atoms, some of which joined up to form molecules of different shapes. Some of these different-shaped molecules in turn, like magnets, attracted similar shaped molecules and so joined up to form larger molecules until they became too large and split into two or more pieces. At some stage, however, a large molecule developed the characteristic of splitting in such a way that the parts retained the same shape as the parent molecule. Each part now continued on its own, growing in size until it in turn split into parts, still retaining the same shape. These molecules were called replicators and with them the process of reproduction had started. The large molecules, including the replicators, continued like magnets to attract smaller 'building-block molecules' to themselves. However resources, even among molecules, are not infinite and when not

many building-block molecules were left, the replicators, started to compete and steal building-block molecules from each other. The competition for resources had started and with it the proto-predators and prey had come into being.

No copying system is absolutely infallible and so some replicators ended up slightly different in shape to the original, either by not splitting into two exactly equal parts or by making a mistake when attracting further building-block molecules. This could make them either weaker or stronger than the original. If stronger, it could give them an advantage in stealing building-block molecules or in resisting others trying to steal their own. Ultimately some replicators may have developed a protective wall of protein around themselves, thus giving birth to the first cells and to life itself.

The first single cells continued to multiply by splitting into equal parts and any variety in form was caused by the occasional mistake. Then a single cell organism discovered sex and as a result the rate of evolution suddenly speeded up. This was because in sexual reproduction each offspring is a unique individual, variety having been produced by mixing the genes from both parents. As before, those with superior qualities were more likely to survive during the competition for resources.

Life was born from conflict and has been dominated by conflict ever since.

As my son and I sat at the edge of the pool we saw a small sponge which intrigued me because it is a living example of the next stage in evolution: single cell organisms joining together to form a community. In prehistory when similar simple communities evolved one stage further, the cells became dependent on one another and formed simple creatures such as jellyfish and polyps. Some polyps subsequently found protection from their predators by covering themselves with limestone, thus forming corals. Other creatures which evolved early on in the sea were flat worms and segmented worms, the first creatures to develop high definition eyes, able to see more than just a difference between light and dark. Subsequently the sea scorpion became a dominant predator, some individuals being giants several metres long.

While these simple creatures evolved, another life form, the blue-green algae, had started to play one of the greatest roles of all in the evolution of life. They developed a way to manufacture food within their own cell walls and they did this by using energy from the sun and extracting hydrogen from the water. By extracting hydrogen from the water, they released oxygen, which, of course, had a major effect on all further development of life. But the blue-green algae played another vital role: from them developed a simple alga with a wax coating which helped it retain moisture. The ability to retain moisture allowed this alga to spread from the sea and on to land. It was the ancestor of mosses and subsequently all land plants.

When the blue-green algae invaded the land, some segmented worms followed, feeding on the algae. They evolved into millipedes, some up to two metres in length. Some segmented worms subsequently developed into predatory centipedes and the equally predatory scorpions had also started to invade the land.

While the insects fed on the land, in the sea evolution produced an amazing variety of creatures. I saw some of them when my son suggested we go for a swim. He had brought some masks and flippers and soon afterwards we were floating among the coral reefs. It was an awe-inspiring sight. Many of the corals, sea anemones and even sea urchins seemed to compete in producing brilliant colours. Yet lurking among them were some that were almost invisible. I realised this when my son touched my shoulder and pointed to a patch of bare sand. At first I could not see anything but then I noticed a small thin, threadlike thing sticking out of the sand. I floated above it to have a better look. Suddenly I noticed two eyes staring up at me. I realised what it was and hastily backed off. It was an enormous stingray. It was most deceptive: previously, I had thought the bare sandy spots were safe, but death lurked here as well as among the colourful corals.

Something touched me. It was my son and he was pointing behind us. I could see a shark. I don't like sharks, perhaps because I feel pretty helpless in water. Luckily this was a small one but I felt uncomfortable enough to suggest that it was lunchtime and so we headed back for the beach.

Later that afternoon we met up with a local fisherman who took us back to the mainland in his narrow canoe. I was sitting in the bow, staring into the clear water, when suddenly I heard a loud splash behind me. I looked around quickly and to my horror saw that my son had fallen overboard, having stood up and slipped. He had managed to grab the side of the canoe and was trying to scramble aboard in extreme haste. Behind him there were three large fins. I rushed over and started to drag him aboard, noticing that the fins close by increased in speed and suddenly submerged. When I had helped Hugo aboard, we watched one of the shapes come towards us under water. I had just seen the film *Jaws* and at that moment I was sure a small canoe was not the right place to be. Then the shape, approaching at speed, suddenly stopped two metres from the boat. I heaved a sigh of relief: it was an inquisitive dolphin!

When we reached the mainland we stopped to visit a small mangrove swamp. I soon spotted what I was looking for: numerous small fish 'walking' on land. As we approached, some of them skipped back to the water but instead of submerging they skipped over the surface of the water at tremendous speed and clambered up the aerial roots of the mangroves. They were mudskippers, which are able to breathe by holding water in their mouths as they rest or pursue their prey on land. It is a superb example of how the first fishes were able to leave the water and colonise land. To be able to remain on land some fishes developed lungs. A living example is provided by a fish which still exists

47

in East Africa. I remember one of my Tanzanian assistants telling me of a friend of his who was digging his garden near Mt Kilimanjaro, about 150 kilometres from the sea, when to his utter amazement he dug up a live fish. This incident apparently caused a considerable amount of excitement in the community for the local people had never heard of such a thing. It is, however, quite common, although apparently not in that area. Lung fish, although normally living in rivers and lakes, can hibernate underground for long periods when small rivers and waterholes dry up during the dry season.

Some of the fish which had moved on to land ultimately developed four legs from their fins and acquired the ability to blink so that they could keep their eyes moist. They had become amphibians and they looked like salamanders. These amphibians had an untapped food supply because the only other creatures on land at the time were the insects. In order to be better able to catch these insects, the amphibians developed an extendable tongue.

The amphibians dominated the land for a hundred million years but most if not all amphibians were dependent on the proximity of water and could not stray far from it. Then the reptiles took over. This coincided with a change in climate which created more arid conditions and the reptiles, by evolving a scaly skin which prevented desiccation, were able to adapt to these conditions by being less dependent on water than the amphibians. In addition the reptiles protected their eggs with a shell, which enabled them to lay their eggs on land rather than in water. Since then some amphibians, such as toads and some tree frogs, have become less dependent on water but they still need it for the development of their young. One species of African tree frog in fact does not lay its eggs in water but instead deposits them on a branch within a protective frothy mass of foam. This branch must be over water, though, so that when the tadpoles hatch they can wriggle out of the frothy mass and drop into the water.

As we drifted in the canoe through the mangrove swamp, we spotted a large monitor lizard crawling along nearby. It was about a metre and a half in length. Without warning a spitting cobra reared up in front of the monitor and we watched fascinated as it spat poison at the lizard's eyes from two metres away. Unlike most creatures, the monitor lizard appears to be immune to the poison and will in fact attack these snakes and eat them. On this occasion, though, the snake quickly slithered up a steep bank, leaving the less agile monitor lizard below. Later we saw a small green snake slowly slide along a branch towards a tree frog. The frog noticed the snake at the last moment and jumped away but the snake struck at tremendous speed and caught the little amphibian in mid-air.

As the amphibians were preyed upon by an increasing number of predators, many developed more extensive protective systems, some becoming camouflaged and others producing extremely powerful poisons. For instance one of the most poisonous creatures in the world is a South American frog from which is derived Tretrodotoxin, an anaesthetic 160,000 times stronger than cocaine.

It was late afternoon by the time we reached Jane's house and we had tea on the beach, looking out over the Indian ocean. It occurred to me that a long time ago this spot was not on the coast but well inland. When the first land formed in prehistory, before life on land began, a number of continents drifted together to form one supercontinent. This was about 200 million years ago. Within this supercontinent, called Pangaea, Madagascar and India were part of what is now East Africa, while Antarctica and Australia were attached to southern Africa; South America was attached to the western side of Africa; and North America and Europe were connected with northern Africa. Thus Africa was the centre of the supercontinent and when the first plants and creatures emerged from the sea it would not have been here, near Dar es Salaam. Over millions of years the numerous evolving creatures colonised the whole supercontinent so that the same fossil dinosaurs and even early forms of mammals have been found on all present day continents. When subsequently the continents drifted apart, many creatures evolved in separate ways and became specific to certain continents; pouched animals are one of the most interesting examples: they are now almost exclusively Australian but were common on the other continents until the placental mammals took over.

While we were having tea the telephone rang. It was Renatus, my mechanic, who informed me that the boat with my new landrover on board had docked. I had regretfully to say goodbye to my son, although he would join me later on the Serengeti for part of his holiday.

The new landrover was beautifully equipped for my work. On the front it had an extremely powerful winch: powerful enough in fact to pull the whole car up a tree. Not that I had any plans to park it in such a place. It would, however, prove useful in getting out of thick mud or soft sand. For photography, I could remove the top half of the door next to the driver's seat and unfold a steel shelf on to which I could mount my tripod heads. In addition I also had a large roof hatch over the front part of the car. This would be useful for observing animals or searching for them: I normally like to be as level as possible with any animals I film and so rarely use a roof hatch for photography except when working with elephants. Inside the back of the car there was a shelf which could be folded out to make a bed and I could insert metal frames with mosquito netting into the windows so that at night I could have plenty of fresh air without being bothered by insects. Finally, rolled up on the roof was an enormous camouflage net with which I could turn the whole car into a hide from which to photograph shy creatures. This camouflage net on a new landrover worried me a bit because I felt the car might be impounded by the army which at the time was at war in Uganda, deposing the dictator Amin. I

OVERLEAF: The length to which a crocodile grows is to a large extent dependent on how much food is available. Due to the abundance of prey animals on the Serengeti some of the largest crocodiles in Africa live there. I saw one which was about twice the length of a full grown hippo and so I estimated some 6 metres long.

therefore hastily acquired a large tarpaulin with which to cover the net.

For some reason I couldn't sleep that night. Through the thin wall of the hotel room I could hear that Renatus was also still awake, so I knocked on his door and suggested that we might as well get an early start for our long journey north. We packed the final things into the landrovers and left Dar es Salaam at two o'clock in the morning, heading north for Arusha, a distance of some 700 kilometres, give or take thirty kilometres or so depending on how many potholes you have to circumvent on the road.

At dawn we were driving parallel to the Usumbara Mountains. I wished we had time to go into these mountains, for the most ancient type of forests in East Africa are to be found there, containing mosses, ferns and the most primitive of all tree types, the tree ferns. These trees, looking like palms but with fern-like leaves on their crowns, can grow up to thirty metres in height.

Before the first trees evolved, the prehistoric mosses gave rise to club mosses which were the first plants to grow roots, enabling them to tap moisture from the soil. In their competition for sunlight some developed into ferns, their expanded leaves better able to collect light. They developed a more solid root system which not only transported water but also anchored them firmly to the ground. As the competition for sunlight continued, some of these ferns started to reach for the sky and so became trees but retained their fern-like leaves.

With the development of trees, the insects evolved quickly: first climbing the trees, then jumping from one to another until some of them developed gliding aids which in turn evolved into wings. The development of rudimentary wings originally had nothing to do with gliding or flying; they were extensions to the body which probably acted like solar panels, helping to collect sunlight and thus warming the insects more quickly. The ability to glide and then fly was of course useful in escaping from the carnivores but some predatory insects followed. Carnivorous dragonflies, with a wingspan of seventy centimetres, soon dominated the sky.

When Renatus and I stopped for coffee early in the morning, I saw a large praying mantis creeping along the branch of an acacia tree. As it moved forward it swayed from side to side like a leaf in the morning breeze. From its movements and body posture it was apparent that it was creeping up on a prey, but I didn't see anything until the mantis's sharply spiked arms suddenly shot forward and grabbed a small camouflaged tree lizard, a gecko, which it ate. Later I watched another predator, a chameleon. It too swayed from side to side as it walked forward. When it got to within twenty-five centimetres of a fly it slowly opened its mouth and then suddenly its long sticky tongue shot forward and caught the fly. I had once seen a chameleon miss its target and hit the branch instead. To my surprise, although the chameleon tugged hard its extended tongue was firmly stuck. Finally it crept forward slowly, tucking its tongue back into its mouth, and only when it reached the spot where it was stuck did it succeed in tugging it loose.

In prehistory the competition between insects, amphibians and reptiles lasted for millions of years and during that time many different species evolved along totally different lines. Among the reptiles, a completely new sort of animal started to emerge, the para-mammals. These were to be the ancestors of all mammals, including man. Astonishingly, this was seventy million years before the age of the dinosaurs.

The para-mammals looked like lizards; they were insect-eaters, and evolved sharp teeth (the precursors of canines) which enabled them to hold on to the wriggling insects before swallowing them whole. They did not, however, grow very large on a diet of insects. Then an enormous change took place: some of them started to eat vegetation. In order to cope with this tough stuff they had to develop larger digestive systems which resulted in an increase in body size. In addition they became munchers rather than swallowing their food whole. They developed jaw muscles. Soon some of their cousins also decided to have a change in their diet, but instead of eating vegetation they ate each other and the herbivores. In order to cope with their large prey, they also grew in size.

Life in those days proceeded at a fairly slow pace: running had not yet been invented, at least among the larger creatures. The early heavy reptiles had legs sticking out of the side of their bodies and anyone who has done push-ups can imagine the effort involved in walking like that, let alone running.

The para-mammals slowly developed legs underneath their bodies. Snakes, of course, went in the opposite direction and lost their legs altogether in order to be able to slide along more quickly. All these creatures were probably cold-blooded but some para-mammals developed enormous 'sails' on their backs which probably acted as solar heaters, much as the early wings had for insects.

One group, the Therapsids, evolved cheekbones and therefore a better jaw articulation which meant they could bit harder and eat more. One group of these developed into Cynodonts or 'Dog Teeth', our direct ancestors. They may have been nocturnal, for some of them had whiskers, probably to aid them in the dark. In order to remain active during cold nights they may have become warm-blooded. If so, they were probably the first warm-blooded creatures on earth and thereby set the scene for the emergence of the mammals. However, one major factor delayed any large scale evolution of mammals for a hundred million years. The age of the dinosaurs started. These creatures became so powerful that they almost exterminated the ancestral mammals.

The dinosaurs had started life as semi-aquatic archosaurs, meaning rulers of reptiles, and they looked and lived very much as crocodiles do today. In order to catch para-mammals coming to drink, the archosaurs increased their speed in water by developing more and more powerful tails and hind legs with which to propel themselves suddenly towards a drinking animal. Probably some

OVERLEAF: Monitor lizards can be two metres in length. Their normal prey is insects but they will also attack and eat snakes and young crocodiles.

53

developed which could maintain this speed, coming out of the water and chasing their prey for a short distance. Because their hind limbs were strong, unlike their forelimbs, and they had a powerful tail to act as a counterbalance, many could run bipedally, as the Australian frilled lizard does today. Now crocodiles, like sharks, are not among my favourite creatures and to imagine a crocodilian creature rushing out of the water at me on its hind legs is enough to send me into a cold sweat. I was not surprised at all to think that these creatures, developing into dinosaurs, made mincemeat out of our ancestors the para-mammals. But as is so often the case, small is beautiful: it was the tiny para-mammals which survived, hiding in forests and remaining or becoming nocturnal. While the dinosaurs roamed the earth the para-mammals existed on insects and to cope with the cold nights became warm-blooded, if they were not so already. They also extended the whiskers which their ancestors had possessed into fur which covered their whole body. Some of these evolved into small shrew-like creatures, the first mammals. Like their reptilian ancestors, however, they continued to lay eggs, as the platypus still does today.

I was thinking about these things as we passed the Usumbara Mountains, but soon afterwards my mind was jerked back to the present and I stopped the car abruptly. A few metres in front of me a large cobra reared up with its hood spread. It soon slid away across the road, however, and disappeared into the bushes. Most people would drive over the unfortunate creature and, given the chance, would kill any snake they see. This is sad because most snakes are harmless and even the poisonous ones try to get out of the way if they can.

When I first arrived in Africa, I was fascinated by snakes and soon thought I knew quite a bit about the African species. As a result I sometimes picked up the harmless ones. One day I was holding a very common small green harmless snake when Jonathan Leakey, a snake expert, arrived on the scene and said,

'Do you know you are playing with a baby boomslang?'

Boomslang means tree snake in Dutch, and they are highly poisonous. That was the last time I handled a snake for fun and I stopped thinking I was an expert. However I did complete a photographic assignment for the National Geographic Society which involved photographing Jonathan Leakey's work with snakes. He had a snake farm where he milked the snake poison which is used to make serum for snake bites. One of the most impressive snakes he had was a Gaboon viper. It was very poisonous, with fangs 2.5 cm long, but it had beautiful and very striking blotches of colour all along its body. I could not believe that this was camouflage until I saw the snake on a forest floor covered with dead leaves: it became almost invisible. While I was photographing this snake, one of Jonathan's African assistants suddenly appeared, out of breath. He had seen a large snake disappear down a burrow about a kilometre away. Jonathan quickly put the Gaboon viper back into its cage, collected some gear and soon we set off for the burrow.

Jonathan strapped a torch around his head, rather like a miner's lamp, and,

holding a sack in front of him, disappeared into the bowels of the earth. He reappeared a little later and said,

'There's a python down there. I'm going down to catch it.'

'Wait,' I said, 'can I get some photographs first?'

'Sure,' he replied, taking the torch from his head and handing it to me. 'The burrow goes straight down about two metres and then makes a right hand turn. The python is just around the corner.'

Soon afterwards I was crawling down the hole. I wanted to see the non-poisonous snake but getting two metres down I thought better of it – I didn't want a struggle with a constrictor – and so just stuck my camera with the flashlight around the corner and took a number of pictures. As I did so, I could hear the snake hissing loudly. Then I crept back to daylight. As I handed the torch back to Jonathan, he said,

'I wouldn't have done that.'

'Why?' I replied, surprised.

'They can bite pretty badly,' he said. 'I always keep a sack in front of me.'

'Thanks for telling me,' I grinned. 'One is always learning something.'

Living in the wild one cannot help getting involved with snakes occasionally. The same is true for almost anyone living in Africa. A friend of mine in West Africa seeing a cobra creep into his MG sports car phoned the police and then watched horrified as they set up a machine gun aimed at his precious car. Luckily the cobra suddenly appeared and slid away into the undergrowth. Another friend, while it was raining outside, entered his garage and to his annoyance continued feeling raindrops. He looked up and searched for the leak in his garage roof. Finally he discovered no leak but a spitting cobra spraying him with poison. Luckily he was wearing spectacles and so his eyes were not affected.

Driving around a bend, I suddenly saw the incredible sight of the snow-capped Mt Kilimanjaro towering 5860 metres into the sky. We were only 150 kilometres south of the equator. Mt Kilimanjaro is in fact an extinct volcano. At least one hopes it is extinct. If a volcano of this size erupted, the consequences could be a disaster of such gigantic proportions that they would make the eruption of Krakatoa in Indonesia, which sent clouds of dust all around the world, seem like a fire cracker.

When we were close to Mt Kilimanjaro we followed a small road which wound its way through the foothills and among banana trees. Just before we reached Marangu, where climbers start their three to five day ascent of the giant mountain, we turned right on to a small muddy track rarely used by cars. A kilometre further on where the track was surrounded by banana trees and coffee bushes we stopped at a small African farm. Here we were warmly greeted by Sirili, who is in charge of my camp on the Serengeti, but who had had some time off to visit his wife and children on his farm. Sirili's wife greeted us as warmly as he had done. She is an amazing lady. Like many African women she runs the farm single-handed while her husband does other work.

Lawrence, my second mechanic, also joined us and we were soon heading west, passing through the small town of Moshi and towards Arusha, ninety kilometres beyond.

OVERLEAF (pp. 60–1): Mt Meru, originally a volcano which blew out one side of its cone, contains a high altitude forest where black and white colobus monkeys bound among lichen-covered trees.

OVERLEAF (pp. 62–3): Elephants pass the snow-covered Mt Kilimanjaro which is a giant volcano, 5860 metres in height.

OVERLEAF (pp. 64–5): Black and white colobus monkeys are leaf eaters. Normally living in thick forests, often at high altitudes, a number of small troops inhabit a riverine forest on the Serengeti.

OVERLEAF (pp. 66–7): Serval cats mainly prey on rodents and birds but can occasionally tackle a Thomson gazelle twice their own size.

2. The Forests

About thirty kilometres before Arusha we turned right on to a dirt track and drove on until we reached the edge of the last remnants of the original forest which covered this area. It is now only a square kilometre in area but forms a final refuge for a troop of colobus monkeys and numerous birds and contains a spring where the water feeds a small stream emerging into an artificial lake. When we got halfway around the forest, we reached a small tourist lodge called Ngare Sero which is owned and run by two friends of mine, Michael and Gisela Leach, and where we would spend the night.

From the comfort of the large verandah of the lodge one can look across a coffee farm and see Mt Kilimanjaro in the distance. The main attractions, however, are the small lake, the beautiful garden and the original forest. Hundreds of birds of many species breed here, tree frogs cling to leaves and numerous spectacular butterflies sip nectar from the colourful flowers so that there is always something interesting to see and admire.

I never miss an opportunity of exploring this tiny forest, so I wandered past the lake where weaver birds were building their intricate nests among the reeds and where a fish eagle, perched on a dead branch, lifted its head to the sky and uttered its spectacular call. Silently I entered the forest. It is no longer big enough to provide a refuge for large creatures, but it is a paradise for numerous spectacular insects.

On a leaf I saw a caterpillar which was camouflaged to look exactly like a bird dropping. Nearby was a more adult form which was much larger and had changed its appearance completely. It had two false eyes painted on its back, making it look from the front like a lizard or snake. I watched as a beetle bumped into it and suddenly a pink protuberance, looking like a snake's tongue, shot out of the caterpillar's neck and touched the beetle which quickly retreated. The tongue-like protuberance contains a poison which, although not deadly, is repulsive. This caterpillar, looking so dangerous, would ultimately turn into a beautiful butterfly, sucking nectar from colourful flowers, transporting pollen and helping the plants to propagate.

I have always been interested in insects and at one time almost decided to specialise in them rather than in larger animals. Their world, when enlarged on film, is incredibly beautiful. At times it can also be horrifying and, surprisingly enough, humorous. I once filmed a small praying mantis, no larger than an ant, as it walked along a branch. It was about to climb up a side twig when suddenly the twig moved slightly. The mantis ran backwards a few steps and stared at the twig. The twig was now motionless, so the mantis walked forward and was

OPPOSITE: Impala normally inhabit bush and woodland but in the Lake Manyara National Park some herds occasionally wander into the forest, the habitat of their ancestors.

69

about to climb up the twig when it again moved slightly. Again the mantis ran backwards and stared intently for quite a while. Once more the twig was absolutely still. This time, however, the mantis very cautiously edged to the side of the branch it was standing on and then very slowly crept past the twig. The twig did not move but when the mantis was almost past, its top bent down and hit the mantis in the rear. The mantis took an enforced flying leap but landed on a nearby leaf. In the meantime the twig had straightened itself again and was motionless. It was a caterpillar, perfectly camouflaged to look like part of the tree.

The variety of caterpillars is enormous, as are the differences in their behaviour. Many are covered by colourful hairs, with each hair containing a protective poison. Normally when the caterpillar pupates it loses these protective hairs. However I have filmed a caterpillar of the Lethe wasp moth which, when ready to pupate, pulls the hairs off its body and sticks these together to form a protective cocoon inside which it pupates.

I once nearly got killed by caterpillars, at least indirectly. One species of hairy caterpillar, called the procession caterpillar, lives in colonies and the individuals sometimes follow each other in single file. They also pupate together and before doing so, they 'sew' together some leaves as a protective covering. However, some ichneumon wasps have very long ovipositors and I have seen these wasps stick their ovipositors far into branches in order to reach grubs inside which they could lay their eggs. I was inquisitive to find out whether any procession caterpillars in a colony had been parasitised. Some thirty kilometres outside Nairobi there was a small valley with a stream, and I knew that these caterpillars fed on trees which grew by the side of a stream. So I wandered through the valley and finally saw, three metres above the stream, a cluster of leaves which had been sewn together along a thick branch. I climbed the tree and edged my way along the branch. I had almost reached the caterpillars when suddenly the branch bent and I was falling head first towards the shallow stream. I knew that I had a good chance of breaking my neck and so I caught my fall with my hands, straining to stop my head hitting the ground. I succeeded to a certain extent, rolling over, but one of my feet hit a rock and I knew I had broken a bone in it. Worse still, in order to break my fall, I had strained just about every muscle in my upper body and could not move enough to scramble up the steep bank and hill. So all I could do was sit in the stream and occasionally shout for help, hoping someone might hear me. My main worry was that I might pass out because of pain, in which case I might drown. I dragged myself to a spot in the bank where there was a bare dry patch on which I could rest my head, still occasionally shouting for help. Finally I was rescued by an African and I spent three weeks in hospital in Nairobi. For the first week I could not turn around in my bed but ultimately my muscles recovered. However, I had only been in hospital for two days when I noticed the nurses repeatedly giggling outside my room. I had the distinct feeling it was something to do with me and so I asked one of them. She replied,

'Do you have to run very fast to catch caterpillars?'

I grinned painfully. 'What makes you ask that?'

She smiled sweetly and explained: 'In the report book it gives the cause of the accident . . . chasing caterpillars!'

Two years later I was lucky not to be locked into a mental institution because of my interest in insects. During the year I had camped in the forest, I had tamed a number of praying mantises and jumping spiders so that they would sit calmly on my hand and take food from my fingers. I had given them all names; a rather dainty white mantis was called Isabella and a colourful jumping spider with large brown eyes was named Sophia. Eight of these creatures accompanied me in my car, each comfortably installed in very large jars with lots of twigs and so on. I had arranged with Dr Leakey to film some of his work at Fort Ternan and I arrived just before sunset to find one of Dr Leakey's assistants, who was a friend of mine, together with a young American student whom I had not met before. Dr Leakey was not due to arrive from Nairobi until the next day. As the sun set, we had some drinks and after that supper. It was while we were having coffee that I said,

'Oh, I must feed my pets.'

I went to the car and soon returned with the jars which I put on the table. The American student looked a bit surprised as I took the pale mantis out of her jar and said,

'I've been worried about Isabella. She hasn't been eating well. Perhaps she didn't like the journey. Maybe she should have a drink first.'

I put Isabella on the table with a drop of water in front of her and took the jumping spider, Sophia, from her jar.

'Of course Sophia has been marvellous. All the time looking out of the window and jumping up and down with excitement whenever she saw a colourful butterfly!'

I was encouraged to exaggerate a bit because out of the corner of my eye I could see the student staring at me in absolute amazement. His conviction that I had been living in the forest for far too long and had become totally unhinged was only reinforced when I produced the remaining six pets and talked lovingly to them for the next half hour. In fact, as with all animals I have watched, each insect was a distinct individual with its own character.

After spending the night at Michael and Gisela's place, I got up early in the morning as I was going to spend a day or so in the higher altitude forests of the Arusha National Park and Mt Meru. I arranged with Renatus and Sirili that they would go into Arusha and start to obtain supplies for our return to the Serengeti and then join Lawrence and me in the late afternoon.

Half an hour later Lawrence and I were driving up a steep and in places rocky track which soon wound its way through a thick forest.

OVERLEAF: Elephant family units, here four, often join up to form larger herds but the family members normally stay close to each other.

71

Now and then we spotted red duikers, pigmy members of the antelope family whose curious Dutch name means 'diver'. Black and white colobus monkeys with their long mantles of pure white hair bounded through the trees or watched us with quizzical expressions. A brilliantly coloured turaco with green body and bright red wings landed on a branch and nearby the sound of two trumpeter hornhills, true to their name, resounded loudly through the forest. Here and there in the forest we passed small blue lakes in which hippos bellowed and lily trotters with long toes waded across lily pads.

After forty-five minutes the forest suddenly thinned out and looking back I could see, far in the distance and several thousand metres below, the flat plains country. To the left Mt Meru still towered a thousand metres above me and just next to me flowed a river, its fast streaming water finding its way among lava boulders, for Mt Meru used to be a volcano: it exploded about two million years ago, blowing out one half of its cone over a wide area. I drove on through bush country and passed a giraffe and two tiny dikdiks, pigmy antelopes no larger than hares.

Not long afterwards we reached two small houses, one of which had belonged to the film star, Hardy Kruger, for whom Sirili had worked many years ago. It was now inhabited by my friends Bert and Stephanie von Mutius and their small son, Daniel. Apart from the two houses and the little Momella Lodge, in the distance, no other buildings were visible. Instead we had a view over a small open plain on which buffaloes grazed and which was surrounded by forest. Beyond that we could see Mt Kilimanjaro, some ninety kilometres away but looking much closer. Just behind us, the snow on the peak of Mt Meru was melting in the sun.

In the evening, I decided to take some sound recordings in the forest. I drove off alone into the darkness and soon reached the forest edge. I continued for two kilometres so that the sound of the fast-streaming river behind me would not affect the recordings, then turned off the road and stopped in a small glade. I reached beside me and put on my earphones, turned the switch of the Nagra recorder and aimed the Sennheiser rifle microphone out of the window. At first all the sounds were of crickets and a cicada in a nearby tree, but then I heard some small creature scuffling through the leaves on the forest floor. There was no way of telling what it was but I imagined it might be a shrew, using the relative safeness of night to move about in search of insects, and this conjured up visions of giant dinosaurs sleeping in the dark forest.

Probably to avoid the dinosaurs, the first mammals, starting as shrew-like creatures, lived in forests and were small and nocturnal. In Africa numerous species of insectivores and rodents still live in trees.

I remember once standing under a palm tree when suddenly it rained pigmy mice. Looking up I saw a poisonous green boomslang or tree snake sliding among the palm leaves. More minute mice leapt from the tree, falling ten metres to the ground. They were so small that at first I thought they were

74

ABOVE AND OPPOSITE: A mother elephant, worried by my close proximity, sniffs the air and then restrains her young calf from following its playmates.

babies but when some of them ran off at high speed, after initially being stunned by the impact with the ground, I realised they were adults. I caught one which seemed to have been hurt by the drop and kept it for a while in a very large jar until it had recovered and could be released. The pigmy mouse is the smallest rodent in the world, growing no longer than 2.5 centimetres. My son, Hugo, was four years old at the time and tremendously excited to watch this tiny mouse feeding, standing on its hind legs and with arms stretched out sideways as far as they could go in order to be able to hold one piece of cornflake.

In addition to extending their whiskers to fur which protected them during their cold nocturnal lives, the first small mammals also developed their senses of smell and hearing, both helpful in the dark. The development of ears was a major evolutionary step. It involved the evolution of the middle ear, a feature unique to mammals, from two tiny bones which had been part of the jaw joint. This separated the ear from the jaw, giving the small mammals and all their descendants the unique ability to hear clearly while eating – something that tree-crunching and bone-cracking dinosaurs would have found difficult. Dinosaurs, in effect, had their ears next to their teeth, which must have been very unpleasant when they were crunching something up!

The development among mammals of the senses of smell and hearing also had the effect of increasing the brain size. All very useful in avoiding dinosaurs. While the dinosaurs still reigned supreme the mammals had already started to diversify into different forms. Some mammals went in the opposite direction to tree tops, namely underground. These included the ancestors of golden moles. The most primitive mammals laid eggs as their ancestors had done and as the platypus and spiny anteater still do. Others started to give birth to live young, either as marsupial mammals, giving birth to tiny offspring which subsequently lived in a pouch as their descendants in Australia do today, or as placental mammals.

Although there was no moon as I sat in the forest, I could see the silhouette of the trees against the sky, which was aglow with stars as is normal in the tropics. Seen from a mountain at high altitude, the stars appeared even brighter than usual. A bat headed towards a moth, but the moth suddenly spiralled erratically through the air and the bat missed. I guessed the moth belonged to a species which can detect the radar signals of bats and so take evasive action in time. This would not have helped it escape from a nightjar, however, for these nocturnal birds lie on the ground, spot the insects silhouetted against the night sky and so pursue them. By day nightjars are superbly camouflaged on the ground, but I once stopped very close to one and watched fascinated as it very very slowly edged away from me, rocking from side to side as if imitating a dead leaf being gently blown by the wind. I have often seen insects use this device but never a bird.

A little later I thought I saw something moving on a branch nearby. I switched on the spotlight attached to the car and saw two bright eyes staring at me from a tree. The eyes, shining like torches, suddenly bounded through the air, landed, then bounded again. It was an extraordinary sight: no body, just the eyes. But I knew it was a bushbaby, a small nocturnal primate which hunts insects and eats fruit. I had always wanted to record their amazingly loud calls and so I switched off the spotlight and turned on the tape recorder, letting the tape run because I wanted the call from beginning to end. Of course I wasn't sure the bushbaby would make its call and so I could only hope for the best, wondering if the tape would run out and the bushbaby would call while I changed reels! Ten minutes later I almost jumped out of my skin: the bushbaby's call drowned the sounds of the crickets. The call is loud at the best of times, but through the powerful microphone it sounded as if the little creature was sitting on my lap.

Insect-eating bats and small primates, the ancestors of today's monkeys, apes and man, evolved before the dinosaurs died out. But life in the early dinosaur-infected forests must have meant that it was prudent for the tree-living mammals to remain up trees as much as possible and when feasible to jump from tree to tree rather than travelling from one tree to another along the ground. As a result, the ability to glide, as flying squirrels and some rodents do today, was an early development. The Lord Derby's flying squirrel of Africa, for instance, is nocturnal and can glide for up to 250 metres, even making 90 degree turns during its flight. Presumably bats, the only flying mammals, also started as gliders. Of course bats evolved a highly efficient radar system, with which some species can spot insects as small as fruit flies. The development of this radar system may have originated with the shrews, who not only use high-pitched squeaks to communicate with each other but also produce high frequency sounds, inaudible to humans, which might be used as a primitive radar system in locating prey, predators or obstacles in its path. While the early bats initially concentrated on insects, some later became fruit eaters. The early primates, in addition to eating insects and fruit, extended their diet to include leaves.

In the dark I could still hear the scuffling through the leaves and, unable to contain my inquisitiveness any more, I briefly switched on my spotlight and saw a hedgehog searching for insects among the dead leaves on the forest floor. It reminded me that a few small mammals had remained on the ground. This ancient insectivorous shrew modified its hairs into prickly spines, a very effective defensive mechanism, while the pangolin, or scaly anteater, developed a protective coat of armour. Both hedgehogs and pangolins are able to roll up into balls as an additional means of defence.

It is rare to see a pangolin and I remember once asking an African tracker if he could find one for me. He looked at me incredulously and said,

'Finding a pangolin is like finding gold.'

Finally, after twenty years in Africa, I saw one and photographed it. It was

LEFT: A young elephant calf must learn to use its trunk and so bends down to drink with its mouth.

ABOVE: A nervous elephant calf sucks the tip of its trunk, just as a nervous human child may suck its thumb.

an extraordinary creature, about a metre long and completely covered in hard scales. As it walked along, it used only its hind legs: it held its front paws with their sharp claws off the ground for most of the time, and used its long and heavy tail as a counterbalance to its body.

Pangolins have long sticky tongues and eat termites, often concentrating on the harvester termite. The soldier harvester termites however, in defence of their nest, squirt a turpentine-like substance at any predators. A pangolin can manage to ignore this when it first starts feeding but as more and more soldier termites gather, the pangolin leaves to find a fresh colony. This is actually advantageous to both prey and predator, because it prevents a termite colony being exterminated and so provides future food for the predator. As I watched the pangolin it was quite obvious that it was rarely seen, for numerous birds gathered around it and stared.

When I told Sirili and the others what I had photographed, they all rushed up to me, repeatedly shaking my hand and congratulating me. According to the local beliefs, seeing a pangolin brings very good luck: I would become very rich that year, they told me, and have many children. I wasn't married at the time and so wasn't sure how delighted they expected me to be with that prediction! A week later, I found another pangolin, a smaller one. In local African folklore to find two pangolins in a week was unheard of and the predictions of how much money I would earn and how many children I would have were beyond belief.

In watching both pangolins, I had noticed small bits missing from their scales. Obviously some predators had tried unsuccessfully to bite into them. I had twice seen hyaenas trying to chew into fairly large tortoises. They too had been unsuccessful but ever since then I have had a good look at any tortoise I come across and have found that quite a large percentage of them have shallow tooth marks on their backs. One tortoise had a big hole in its back, penetrating past the scales and with the bone shell below shattered. Amazingly, though, a completely new bone had started to form underneath the old one and I knew it would eventually be covered by new scales.

Nobody knows why the dinosaurs died, but the small mammals suddenly and fortuitously lost their major predators and were able to take over the world. Some emerged from their underground havens while others joined them from the trees. With the world at their disposal, they soon diversified into many forms. They still had some enemies left, however, for one group of dinosaurs had certainly survived: those that had developed into the birds. These took over the predatory niche left by their ancestors, the dinosaurs, and some became powerful carnivores. Some grew to over two metres in height, and, with their enormously powerful legs and massive beaks, must have terrorised the small mammals. These birds, with no enemies to fear, lost the power of flight. This was their undoing, for the small mammals soon evolved into larger forms, including a carnivorous group called the creodonts, and they exterminated most of these large flightless birds. Since then it has been prudent for most birds to remain in the air.

The creodonts had already started to evolve by the time the dinosaurs became extinct. Although they are not the ancestors of today's carnivores, they evolved along very similar lines to them and included creatures similar in appearance and presumed habits to mongooses, civets, badgers, wolves and cats. Starting as small predators some of them grew in size: one large species in Africa, similar to a hyaena in habits, weighed about 800 kilograms and had a skull 60 centimetres in length, which makes it about the size of a grizzly bear. These predators had one major problem: they had small brains. This ultimately led to their extinction, for they were unable to keep up with the evolution of their prey, who were becoming swifter and more accomplished at developing escape strategies.

The balance between survival and extinction is a fine one. For a prey species to survive, it must evolve ahead of its predators, but if the predator species is to survive, it cannot afford to stay too far behind. Among present day mammals in Africa, it is striking how often healthy, full grown prey escape; the predators mainly seem to catch the sick, the old and the young. Interestingly, by catching the sick, the predators are presumably helping the evolution of their prey, leaving the healthy ones to breed.

The ancestor of all carnivores was a small tree-living nocturnal animal called Miacis. The miacids superseded the creodonts because of their more advanced and adaptable teeth – and bigger brains, which enabled their hunting techniques to adapt to the different types of prey. From this primitive creature arose the two great carnivore groups: the cats and the dogs. Fossils are so scanty that it is not known how these two groups developed from the early miacids. Perhaps the dogs developed in the temperate north (where colder and more open habitats favoured co-operative hunting and group living), and the cats in the tropical forests.

The earliest cats would have been similar to genets in form and lifestyle. Living in dark, thick forests, they would have been small, solitary, nocturnal, and camouflaged with spots and/or stripes. The genet is a small slender-bodied creature, spotted like a leopard, with short legs and a long tail. It is a tree-climbing creature par excellence. As I sat in the forest, I saw one climb down a tree head first. Once on the ground it caught and ate an insect. Then it sat still, listening, its agile ears moving back and forth until they both concentrated on one spot in the grass. The genet silently walked forward and suddenly grabbed a small green snake which it also ate.

I have seen quite a few small carnivores catch snakes and have often wondered if they are immune to the poison or able to tell in some mysterious way which are poisonous and which are not. Jackals will calmly pick up some snakes and eat them, and yet fight and kill other snakes first, taking great care to jump aside each time the snake strikes with its fangs. The genet I was watching had picked the snake up by its tail. If the snake had been poisonous, it would have had plenty of opportunity to turn around and bite the genet. Instead, it just tried unsuccessfully to wriggle away. Later, when the genet had disappeared up another tree, I saw a slender mongoose, also a snake eater and similar in body build to the genet but without spots. Although the mongooses, of which there are many species, and the genets, do catch and eat snakes, they normally feed on insects, lizards, rodents and so on. The mongooses evolved in a different way to their genet-like cousins by spending more time on the ground, although the slender mongoose is agile in trees. Today, when danger threatens, a genet normally will try to find refuge up a tree, while mongooses will flee along the ground.

This slender mongoose was sitting on a log; it looked straight at me for a while, then twisted its agile body around and disappeared along the log, so smoothly that it almost appeared to be sliding along.

It was close to midnight in the forest and so I switched off the tape recorder, happy with my recording of the bushbaby. I started the car and turned back towards Bert and Stephanie's house.

Next morning, after breakfast, I set off in the new landrover to drive up a tiny winding track which leads a long way up Mt Meru. While the peak of Mt Meru is bare and occasionally covered in snow, a beautiful forest covers most of the mountain slopes, including in places bamboo forest. Being a high altitude forest where it is often quite cold, it is very different to the African forests in which I lived for many years. I wanted to spend a day in the forest and watch some of the creatures which inhabit it. All around, as I drove up the steep track, I saw a profusion of moss covering the ground, and pallid green lichen, called 'old man's beard', hung from the boughs and swayed gently in the breeze. Lichen is an interesting growth for it consists of two separate organisms: algae, sometimes blue-green algae, the ancestor of all plants, together with fungus. In many cases the two have become dependent on each other and thus cannot exist on their own.

The track leading up Mt Meru is so steep in most places that I had to keep the car in four wheel drive. In one place a giant fig tree straddles the track so that one passes underneath it, among tremendous roots. Every now and then I crossed small clear streams. At one point I saw two bushbucks, both females, without horns, and I guessed they were a mother and her almost fully grown daughter. The daughter was feeding from the lush vegetation but the mother was lying almost motionless on top of a moss-covered rock. From there, she had a good view over the surrounding forest. I looked at her through binoculars and could see she was calmly chewing her cud.

As the ungulates started to feed on vegetation in the forest, the plants tried

84

TOP: Banded mongooses forage for insects, birds' eggs, lizards and occasionally snakes. A pair of captive banded mongooses which I tested threw stones at a hard shelled ostrich egg and I suspect that various mongoose species will ultimately be discovered to be tool users.

BOTTOM: A caracal (African lynx) lies absolutely still while watching some rodents, their normal prey. They may also tackle dikdik and Thomson gazelles.

to defend themselves by producing poisonous substances, as some had already done to protect themselves against insects and other early plant eaters. Possibly in order to detoxify these poisons many mammalian plant eaters evolved a digestive system which included pre-gastric fermentation. Thus the ruminants, which include cows, gulp down their food; it is then pre-digested and detoxified in the stomach before being regurgitated for chewing and returned to the stomach. This adaption gives the ruminants a wider choice of diet, allowing them to exploit more fibrous foods. It also helps as a protection against predators because the ruminants can spend less time gathering food in potentially dangerous spots, and more time chewing it in a safer place.

Most forest-living mammals tend to be solitary creatures. That is to say, although some may live in pairs, both the male and the female tend to wander around alone most of the time within their territory. There are various reasons for this. First of all, surprising though it may seem, specific food plants in a forest are often sparsely distributed and ungulates rarely eat the complete plant, usually only selecting succulent morsels from each. This makes it impractical for them to live in large groups. Also, if prey animals lived in groups they would more easily be spotted and tracked by predators. In open country, the opposite occurs: a lone ungulate is in any case easy to spot in open country and unable to hide, so it makes sense for them to live in herds and have as many eyes as possible looking out for predators. In addition, ungulates in open country are usually grazers, feeding on grass which commonly grows close together. Some ungulates in forests also live in herds, such as buffalo, but they too are grazers and I suspect their ancestors were originally open country animals which returned to the forest but retained their herd-living habit. It is noticeable, however, that their herd sizes are smaller than in open country.

Animals which can climb and live in tree tops in the forest have a larger quantity of food available than those on the forest floor. Thus monkeys can live in troops and have the advantage of more eyes looking out for danger. The relationship between body size, being solitary or living in family groups or troops, and of course food supplies and size of territory, is finely balanced: some very large primates, such as orang utans, are solitary while gorillas live in troops and chimpanzees do both: they often wander around alone or in family groups but occasionally join up together, especially when large amounts of food, such as one or more fruiting trees, are available in one spot.

I drove on. Finally the track turned out of the forest and ended in a small open space. I took some binoculars and walked up a little track which led further up the mountain and into a forest where the floor and lower trunks of the trees were covered in thick moss and white lichen hung from branches, swaying gently in the breeze.

I hadn't got more than a few hundred metres when I caught sight of a leopard. I hid among the buttresses of a large tree. Peering cautiously around the tree, I realised that the leopard had not noticed me and then I saw why: its full

OPPOSITE: A dwarf mongoose on sentry duty, having seen potential danger, warns its companions with shrill calls.

attention was concentrated on a red duiker grazing peacefully in a small glade about fifty metres away. The leopard slowly walked forward, staring hard at its prey. Suddenly, without warning, the duiker looked up. The leopard had, however, reacted instantly, freezing in mid-stride, one front paw in the air. For a while the duiker stared all around, then lowered its head and continued to graze. The leopard waited a second, then silently moved forward again. This time it held its body slightly lower than before. It had barely gone a metre when the duiker again suddenly looked up. Maybe the leopard had reacted less quickly this time, for the duiker stared straight at it without looking around. At first the leopard remained absolutely motionless but then, millimetre by millimetre, and so slowly it was almost unnoticeable, the leopard lowered its body towards the ground. The duiker continued to stare and I felt sure it had seen the predator. Two minutes later the leopard's tummy touched the ground and soon afterwards its chin. It sank still lower until its body was almost flat. For a while the duiker continued to stare but then it finally lowered its head to graze once more. The leopard slowly raised itself very slightly and crept forward, its tummy brushing the forest floor. During the next ten minutes the duiker frequently looked up but the leopard always reacted instantly and the duiker apparently saw nothing. Finally the leopard got to within twenty metres of the antelope, close enough to charge with little chance of its prey escaping. But the leopard apparently wanted to make absolutely sure of a successful kill and as it crept closer still, I felt tense and held my breath. Suddenly an earpiercing scream resounded close to me. I froze. Then I realised it was a monkey. Both the leopard and the duiker had reacted instantly and I could see the antelope running for its life with the leopard in close pursuit. At first the antelope ran straight but then suddenly it started zigzagging fast and erratically among trees and bushes and low vegetation. In doing this it gained some ground on the leopard and then suddenly, when briefly out of sight of the cat, it literally dived to the ground – hence its name – and remained absolutely motionless, hidden among some vegetation. The leopard stopped running and with cold yellow eyes stared briefly up at the Sykes monkey which screamed its alarm calls incessantly. Then the leopard ignored the monkey and wandered zigzagging among the vegetation, trying to find the duiker's hiding place. It continued to do so for fifteen minutes and then, through persistence and chance, it finally approached the spot where the duiker was hiding. I could not see the antelope but I thought that, being among thick vegetation, it could not possibly see the leopard getting closer. Yet I could imagine its nose twitching as it sniffed the air and its sensitive ears listening to each rustling leaf whenever the monkey above paused in its warning calls. Finally one of its senses told it that the leopard was very close and it jumped up and raced away again, once more pursued by the leopard. The duiker had presumably lived in this part of the forest for most if not all of its life, occupying a much smaller territory than the leopard, and so probably knew every tree and bush and peculiarity of the

terrain. In any case it made full use of all possible obstacles as it zigzagged through the forest and once again managed to increase the distance between itself and the leopard. Again, when it was out of sight of the cat, it dived to the ground, this time in a depression which was well covered by vegetation. As before, the leopard stopped and then continued its search. I had once seen a leopard on the Serengeti search for a young gazelle in this fashion for forty-five minutes until it was successful. This time, however, the leopard gave up after twenty minutes, possibly disturbed by the continued alarm calls of the Sykes monkey. Soon afterwards the leopard disappeared among the lichen-covered trees and moss-covered rocks. The monkey stopped screaming and bounded away along tree-top branches.

The forest was silent once more but for the courting calls of crickets. I waited for half an hour but the duiker was cautious and did not move and so finally I crept away.

Duikers are similar in build to the ancestors of all antelopes and probably similar in behaviour too. If this is so then the escape strategy of the duiker, zigzagging, diving to the ground and remaining motionless, was probably an ancient behaviour pattern. Hiding and remaining motionless are of course ideal escape strategies in a forest where dense vegetation and dark areas are often available.

On my way back through the forest, I saw a male bushbuck lying on top of a moss-covered rock. It gave him a perfect view over the surrounding forest and I was reminded of the behaviour of the topi, one of the hartebeest family, which often stand on the top of termite mounds in open country and are rarely caught by lions. The bushbuck, however, was combining a good view with remaining motionless and, although not as well hidden as the duiker had been, was still quite difficult to see. Bushbuck sometimes associate with baboons which have tremendously sharp eyesight and are therefore quick to spot danger and, like the Sykes monkey, raise the alarm.

I have always been fascinated by the relationships between different species. I was once watching a troop of banded mongooses as they searched for insects. A bushbuck emerged from the small riverine forest and started to graze among the banded mongooses. To my surprise one of the small mongooses leaped up, grabbed the bushbuck's tail in its mouth and hung on. The bushbuck reacted as if in fright, quickly lowering its rump, and the mongoose let go. Instead of running away, however, the bushbuck daintily walked away a little distance and then continued to graze, but the mongoose had followed it and again leaped up and hung on to the buck's tail for a while. This time the bushbuck lowered its rump more slowly, but continued to graze completely unconcerned. I came to the conclusion that this bushbuck had experienced this 'game' before.

By the time I got back to the car it was getting late. In the forest the evening chorus of black and white colobus monkeys and trumpeter hornbills echoed among the trees and up valleys until they mingled with the sounds of mountain

streams and waterfalls. The setting sun had turned the snow of Kilimanjaro pink and deep shadows were falling over the country below.

The next morning we said goodbye to Bert, Stephanie and Daniel and drove off in convoy into the forest and towards the open country below. The trailer was attached to my car and Sirili, Renatus and Lawrence followed in the old landrover. As we drove through the green forest we occasionally passed small blue lakes where lily trotters with long toes waded across lily pads. Providing they did not stay too long on each large leaf, it would hold their weight, but whenever they paused to catch an insect, the leaf would slowly sink under them and they would quickly walk on across other leaves. We stopped at one lake and watched hippo heads emerge and snort sprays of water into the air and then we listened to them bellowing their territorial calls. In a small opening in the forest a bushpig with four young appeared and rolled in the mud near the edge of the lake. They and the hippos are distantly related and probably started life in landscapes very similar to this.

Although giant forest hogs, tremendous creatures weighing up to 250 kilograms, do not occur in this forest, I have seen them in the Aberdare Mountains in Kenya. I had watched fascinated as five of them confronted a buffalo on a salt lick. The buffalo had wisely made way. These were, however, small creatures compared to some of the prehistoric forms, which included pigs the size of rhinos with tusks a metre long and buffalo-like creatures almost twice that size with horn spans of about three metres.

We hadn't driven much further when we saw a strange sight: four giraffes feeding in the thick forest. Giraffes are open country animals and it occurred to me that if these individuals were left to propagate over the next million years or so, they would turn into a different species, possibly resembling okapis to which they are related and which used to be more like giraffes in appearance.

Finally the forest made way for bush country where we saw many more giraffes. An hour later we drove into the small town of Arusha and stocked up on supplies. Soon afterwards we were heading toward the forest of Lake Manyara, a distance of some 150 kilometres.

For the first hundred kilometres we drove on tarmac with an occasional pothole but then turned right on to a dirt road which was badly corrugated and rough. After forty-five kilometres we passed through a stretch of open country. A large cobra was sunning itself on top of a termite mound and we saw pigmy mongooses peering from others. Soon afterwards we were driving along the edge of the Lake Manyara forest with its enormous trees and towards the steep wall of the Gregory Rift where giant baobab trees, some three thousand years old, stand like sentries, overlooking the Lake Manyara National Park. We did not proceed up the rift but turned on to a track to the left which led through a small part of the forest to the entrance of the park. Here we were greeted by the wardens as long lost friends: some years earlier we had lived here for five months while I photographed elephants. We chatted for a while with the wardens, and obtained our permits to camp in the park for a few days: I was keen to see the elephants again. Soon afterwards we were erecting our tents in the forest, watched by a troop of Sykes monkeys and baboons.

It was close to sunset by the time we were ready to collect firewood, taking care when lifting the dead logs not to put our hands on any scorpions. On a previous visit, my son had been stung by a scorpion and the experience had been a frightening one: the extremely painful poison had shot up his arm and down the right side of his chest, making breathing difficult. In desperation we had driven fast up the Gregory Rift to the Lake Manyara Hotel in the forlorn hope that we might find a doctor among the tourists there. A Tanzanian doctor happened to be spending the night in the hotel and, amazingly, had the required medicine with him which he injected into Hugo's hand. Five minutes later most of the pain was gone and gradually he was able to breathe more easily. Normally, I have a full medical kit with me in the car in addition to a less extensive first aid kit but at the time we had just arrived back from England and the full medical kit had been stored in the camp on the Serengeti during my absence. Ever since then it never leaves the car except to treat someone.

The one major worry when living in the wild far away from doctors and hospitals, as we do on the Serengeti, is that one of us might have a serious accident. I have had to treat others, including five soldiers whose landrover overturned; I thought one of them would die, but luckily he survived. I have myself been lucky, in spite of being accident prone when I was a teenager. Maybe it made me more careful as I grew older. Be that as it may, I did once nearly lose an eye. I was walking through the forest with Jane while we were working on chimpanzees, when a branch, which had been bent aside, suddenly whipped back at me. I felt a twig go straight into my eye and break off at the end. I contorted briefly then put my fingers to my eye and could feel an inch of twig sticking out. Jane looked back and told me later she had nightmares for a long time afterwards. The twig was firmly wedged into my eye and I remember that my first feeling was one of surprise that it did not hurt more. Convinced I would be blind in one eye, my second thought was relief that it was my left eye and not the one I use for photography. Any medical help was far off and so I decided that in any case I had to pull the twig out. So I braced myself and pulled. An extraordinary sensation followed. I could feel that the twig had penetrated right into the socket and in doing so had pushed my eye back to front. As I pulled the twig out, my eye rolled back to its correct position. Amazingly, apart from a tiny red mark, there was nothing wrong with it.

As we had supper in the open air we watched the twinkling light of stars above us and of numerous fireflies in the forest around us. One landed on a book and I could clearly read the text by its light. There are many species of firefly and each uses a different 'morse' signal to attract a mate of the same species. One

OPPOSITE: Unaware of the proximity of lions, a herd of elephants grazes calmly. When elephants notice lions the family members bunch protectively around their small calves.

species of female firefly, however, after being mated, changes her signals to those of a different species and having attracted males of that species to her alluringly lit posterior, grabs and eats them.

Now and then I could hear elephants in the forest as they fed and as family members kept contact with each other by 'tummy rumbling', an accurate description of the sound. When I first started watching these gigantic creatures, the main thing I noticed was how very gentle they normally were, not only with each other but also when much smaller creatures, such as baboons, were wandering almost among their feet. During such times they appeared to move more slowly and cautiously as if aware that, with their huge strength, any sudden movement could cause death and destruction.

The closest living relatives to elephants are hyraxes, which live in trees or on rocks. They are small furry creatures similar to rabbits in appearance but with short round ears. Seacows such as manatees and dugongs are also related to elephants. Their ancestors were the size of a pig and lived in marshes. Originating in Africa, they spread into Europe, Asia and America. Those which grew in size to become elephants or elephant-like creatures included some with tusks in both upper and lower jaws and others with tusks pointing downwards. Although hyraxes are now small, some prehistoric forms were important herbivores growing to the size of a pony in Europe, while in Africa one evolved the size of a rhino.

I remembered an occasion when I was camping with some friends from Europe. It was about three hours after sunset and we were sitting around the camp fire. Earlier we had heard lions roaring and hyaenas giggling hysterically, but for the past hour it had been almost silent except for the sound of crickets. Apart from a small circle of light created by the flickering flames of the fire, it was pitch dark. Suddenly, a few metres away and without warning, the most blood-curdling screams shattered the silence. My friends froze in horror. I can only describe the sound as being like the cry of a pig being slowly throttled. In fact it was the healthy call of a little tree hyrax, seeking a mate or proclaiming its territory. If its prehistoric, rhino-sized relative made a sound like that, I imagine the trees would have trembled and the call would have been audible for forty kilometres or more.

No such alarming call disturbed us now and I went to bed looking forward to renewing my acquaintance with the elephants I had got to know some years before.

Early next morning, I drove into the park. I had only gone 500 metres when I passed the spot where I had once found a rhino with a Maasai spear right through it. It was still alive when I found it. It lifted its head slightly, looked at me, and then died. It was sickening to see a great creature killed so that its horn could be used either as a supposed aphrodisiac or to make handles for daggers sold in Arab countries.

Over twenty years ago I joined the Kenya Game Department for a while as

96

a honorary game warden. During that time I assisted Nick Carter who was saving rhinos from heavily poached areas and moving them into national parks. Nick was nicknamed 'Carter the Darter' because he used a crossbow to shoot an arrow with a hypodermic needle containing a drug. He had a red, well-trimmed beard, and wore a hat which made him look like Robin Hood. Nick was frighteningly accurate with the crossbow and I once saw him make a hit from well over a hundred metres. However, with most rhinos, we got to within a few metres, either by car in open country, or just by creeping up on them. It made me realise how easy it must be to hunt these short-sighted creatures. Our main problem was that the drug took about ten minutes to immobilise the rhino. During that time it could run a considerable distance and so we had to follow, usually on foot and guided by trackers from the Wakamba tribe who could follow a rhino's spoor even over rocky ground – a quite extraordinary feat. Even when the drug began to take effect, the rhino sometimes remained standing, and so we had to creep up and quickly tie its hind legs. It was vital that we reached the drugged rhino quickly: the drug used in those days affected the respiratory system and we had to give the rhino oxygen. Sometimes, as we crept up on the rhino and were about to tie its hind legs, we would find that the drug had not taken complete effect and the rhino would naturally turn around and charge. Needless to say, we all fled for the nearest trees. Sometimes, the closest tree was rather large and I remember one of the trackers, with the rhino close on his heels, taking a flying leap for such a tree and clinging on like a limpet. His arms barely spanned a quarter of the tree, but he was encouraged to cling on since the rhino had stopped below him and was stabbing its horn at his bottom, only missing it by centimetres. A similar scene is accurately portrayed by dummies in the jungle trip in Disneyland. Luckily we managed to distract the rhino from the unfortunate man but all the same he remained stuck to the tree until the rhino fell over, fast asleep, a minute later.

I continued through the Lake Manyara National Park and stopped at a spot which gave a good view. Through my binoculars I saw what I was looking for: the elephants were descending the slopes of the Gregory Rift and soon reached an area of acacia trees from which they fed. I drove the car in their direction but didn't get too close. Instead I parked the car in their path, allowing them to decide how close it was safe to come. Luckily they did not seem worried and were soon all around me, some within ten metres. I watched them and took an occasional photograph, concentrating on a tiny calf.

The calf was watching a white egret which was searching for insects disturbed from the grass by the elephants' feet. Suddenly the calf ran at the egret with wiggling trunk. The bird ignored the calf and continued to feed. The little elephant stopped in its tracks, stared with its ears out and nervously put the tip of its trunk in its mouth, just as a child may suck its thumb. The bird briefly chased an insect and the calf hastily retreated between its mother's legs, from where, still sucking the tip of its trunk, it watched the bird. The bird finally flew off, landing close to some other elephants, and the tiny calf emerged from between its mother's legs. This time, wildly wiggling its trunk again, it went up to another, somewhat larger calf and butted it as if inviting it to play. To my surprise, the older calf reacted quite violently, butting the tiny calf so hard that the youngster almost lost its balance. This time, however, the tiny calf did not suck the tip of its trunk. Instead it seemed livid, dashing back and forth in front of the older one, shaking its little head and wiggling its tiny trunk erratically in every conceivable attitude as an attempted threat. The older calf took no notice and the tiny calf became more and more vigorous with its threats. Then it tripped and fell, but it still contrived to shake its trunk at the older calf, like a snake appearing above the grass. The older calf continued feeding as if the tiny calf did not exist. Finally the tiny calf got up, went over to a small log and gave it a temperamental kick.

At first I could only see fifteen elephants but slowly more family herds appeared, each led by a matriarch, until there was a total of about a hundred individuals. I saw two adults from different families approach each other and greet by putting the tips of their trunks into each other's mouths: it reminded me of kissing in humans. Gentle physical touch is reassuring in both man and elephants and elephants may gently touch one another when frightened, just as humans do.

Young elephants have to learn how to use their trunks. When drinking water, for instance, young calves bend right down and drink with their mouths. Even when grabbing twigs or playing, the young calves do not seem to have complete control over their wiggly noses: the trunks seem to have a life of their own. I remember watching one young calf tread on the tip of its trunk and, not surprisingly, come to a complete standstill. It had no idea how to rectify the situation. Instead of lifting its foot, it pulled and tugged at its trunk as hard as possible, like a blackbird pulling at a resisting worm. Finally, apparently without realising what it was doing, it lifted its foot slightly. As a result its trunk suddenly shot loose and the calf tumbled over backwards.

Throughout the day I followed the elephants. Just before midday they went to a small stream and drank. As the adults drank, the little calves bathed, sometimes going completely underwater with only the tips of their trunks sticking out like a snorkel. Later, they had a mud bath and afterwards two elephants picked up sticks and used them as tools to scratch between their forelegs, a behaviour pattern I have often seen in this park, although it has only rarely been reported in scientific literature.

Mud bathing undoubtedly helps elephants to keep cool and may also help to protect them against biting insects. Staying cool is important because overheating is fatal. The elephant's large ears are in fact a highly efficient cooling system. Warm blood entering the ears from the body is cooled by as much as 10 degrees Centigrade before it enters the body again. The cooling efficiency is further increased when an elephant fans its ears as it often does and when it squirts water over its ears. An elephant overheating in open country may, in an emergency, poke its trunk down its throat, suck up some stomach juices and squirt these behind its ears.

I am sure the wrinkles on an elephant's skin are another cooling device, for each wrinkle creates a small shadow. The same system is used on camera bodies.

As I watched the elephants, a large bull looked at me and slowly rocked his front foot back and forth. I knew it was a hesitant threat: he wasn't quite sure whether to approach or retreat. Finally he decided to charge, slowly, with his ears held out wide. I didn't move and this obviously unsettled him, for he stopped a few metres from the car, towering above it and looking down at me. I remained motionless and ultimately, as a final threat, the elephant shook his head violently so that his ears audibly slapped the side of his body and head. Then he wandered off a short distance and continued to feed. I knew this bull elephant well. Previously, when I had watched the elephants, he had threatened me almost every time we met. But it was always bluff. Yet, if I had driven away, he would have chased me, encouraged that he had the upper hand. Of course some elephants are not bluffing and I would not advise anyone to go too close to elephants without having got to know the individuals from a distance first. In the Lake Manyara Park there used to be some elephants which charged almost on sight and it was no bluff, as Ian Douglas Hamilton, who studied elephants there, found to his cost. They destroyed his landrover and he was lucky to escape. There is no doubt in my mind that these elephants had had a bad experience with man in the past, possibly having lost family members in hunting incidents, or even having a bullet embedded into their own bodies. One wonders how many innocent people have been killed by animals wounded by hunters. Of course, even knowing individual elephants is no guarantee of safety, since, as in man, moods can change.

I remember once following a family herd of elephants which contained a female with three calves, one of which was only a few weeks old. The mother had extraordinary tusks for, apart from being long, they curved towards each other so that the points met and almost seemed fused together. Renatus, my mechanic, had joined me that day because we had agreed that he would give me some lessons to improve my Swahili while the elephants rested in the heat of the day. We had been threatened by the same bull I mentioned earlier and I think Renatus was coming to the conclusion that I was a bit crazy and regretting he had agreed to accompany me during my work. He seemed quite relieved when, as the sun started to set, I suggested we should return to camp.

In order not to give elephants a fright, I would never drive off immediately after starting the car engine but always let the engine run for a little first, thus giving the elephants plenty of warning that the car was about to move. This time I started the engine. But I had barely taken my hand off the key when I

noticed the female elephant with the extraordinary tusks charging towards us at full speed. I knew instantly that this was no bluff: her trunk was tucked between her legs, her head was held high and the single point where her tusks met was pointed straight at us. She was within thirty metres and I hastily put the car into first gear and shot away along a small sandy track. I kept my one hand on the gear lever, planning to change into second as soon as I had built up enough speed. I was about to do so when I glanced at Renatus sitting next to me. He was staring out of the back of the car, eyes wide with terror. I looked back and shall never forget what I saw. The elephant was towering above the rear of the car in a cloud of dust, the single tip of her tusks within a metre of the rear window, and beyond them I could see her small eyes staring down at us. I knew I couldn't afford the slight drop in speed which would occur if I changed gear. Instead I transferred my hand from the gear lever and gripped on to the steering wheel with both hands, waiting for the impact which was bound to come. If I could keep the car on the small track, we could probably get away with only damage to the rear, but if the impact threw the car off the track we would end up among thick bush and at the mercy of the elephant and the family group which I knew would soon join her. To my amazement the impact never came. Maybe the dust thrown up by the car had helped or maybe the speed of the six-cylinder engine had just been enough to keep us ahead. In any case we had had a very narrow escape. I turned to Renatus and joked,

'I just missed the most incredible picture. In future you had better do the driving so that if this happens again, I can get a photo out of the roof hatch.'

This totally convinced him I had gone crazy. Horrified, he replied,

'Please, I never want to come into this park again.'

Selfishly I decided to use the situation and said,

'Okay. But you can see how much my life depends on you. If the car hadn't started immediately we wouldn't be talking to each other!'

Although Renatus and Lawrence had always looked after the vehicles well, Renatus had been a little slack lately, having discovered that the beautiful young ladies of Mto wa Mbo, the nearby village, found him rather handsome. From that moment on, whenever I returned from a day's work, Renatus and Lawrence dived under the car and inspected it from top to bottom before leaving for the local dance where they proudly spread rumours of their strange boss who let elephants surround and touch his car. A friend of mine, Brian Jackman of *The Sunday Times*, experienced this when he joined me on a safari. Brian had watched elephants many times before, having made various trips to different parts of Africa, but when he was with me, we were surrounded by two family herds. While one elephant approached the front of the car and stretched its trunk towards the window, another started sniffing the back of the car. All we could do was remain motionless until finally, having satisfied their curiosity, the elephants wandered off and continued feeding.

Once, when I was parked among the herd of about a hundred elephants, a female passed between the front of the car and a tree. I was surprised, as there was little space between the two. Her calf, four weeks old or so, started to follow but then approached the front of the car. It was so small that I did not see it until I noticed a small trunk wriggling and sniffing over the front of the bonnet. At first the mother did not notice but then she looked around, turned fast and stared as if in disbelief. I held my breath. I was in a dangerous position, completely hemmed in by elephants with a large bull only three or four metres away on one side. The mother elephant's ears came out, a sure sign of alarm or threat, and I shall never forget what happened next. She literally tiptoed over, stretched her trunk as far as it would go, wrapped it around the calf's back and gently pulled it away.

Small calves can put one into difficulties at the most unexpected moments. One day I was photographing two family units which had joined up to drink from some small holes dug into soft sand. While the adults drank, two small calves started to play together. Eventually one family unit had drunk enough and moved away, circling close past my landrover before heading toward the bushes about a hundred metres away. The two calves, still engrossed in their game, followed. This surprised me, for one calf was moving unusually far from its own family, which had remained drinking. I suspected it had not realised what was happening and thought both families had left together. This was confirmed a minute later. The calf suddenly stopped, stared at the adults it had been following, then turned and looked back. Unfortunately for the calf, my car stood between it and its family, who were therefore hidden from sight. Unfortunately for me, the calf apparently thought I must have quickly gobbled up its whole family and, with earpiercing squeals, it charged me. Even more unfortunately for me, the adults on the other side, hearing the squeals, as if coming from inside my car, started to charge from the opposite direction. There was no time for me to start the car and get out of the way. At the last moment however, the calf, having almost reached the landrover, circled the car. As soon as the adults saw it, they stopped and, much to my relief, calmed down as the calf joined them unhurt. Soon afterwards the calf was standing underneath its mother, staring back at me and sucking the tip of its trunk.

One would think that elephants had nothing to fear from other predators than man. I feel sure, however, that lions occasionally take calves and as a result elephants can be very wary of lions. I remember once watching a large herd of elephants as they fed close to a small river. Suddenly one of them started trumpeting loudly and running back and forth. Moments later the adult elephants of each family group stood packed together, their calves protectively in their midst. Almost at the same time three lionesses with three cubs sneaked out of the bushes close to me. Then one of the lionesses looked around, stopped, called softly and went back towards the elephants. I wondered what she was up to, but a moment later she emerged again, followed by a fourth cub which had obviously got lost in the confusion of trumpeting elephants. Then all the lions calmly waded across the river away from the elephants. For the next hour, however, the elephants were very restless and the family members stayed close together. Some weeks later I followed a fairly large elephant calf which had apparently lost its family. It was finally eaten by lions and, although I did not see it, I am reasonably sure the lions actually killed it.

Early in the morning after my day watching the elephants, we broke down the simple camp in the forest and loaded all our gear into the landrovers. Then we drove into the village of Mto wa Mbo where we bought some final supplies from the market. Once this was completed with much bargaining by Sirili we headed up the Gregory Rift. Numerous baboons were sitting along both sides of the rough road. They eyed the bunches of bananas on our roof rack eagerly but we were going too fast for them to risk jumping on to the car. Baboons can be quite cheeky and aggressive and I don't know how the locals manage to pass them when carrying their wares on their head. People sometimes throw food out to baboons from the safety of their cars, thinking they are doing them a favour. The opposite is true, for this encourages the baboons to become more cheeky and they may well attack an innocent passerby. This may result in the warden shooting some baboons in retaliation.

We finally reached the top of the rift and from then on our journey was through undulating farm country as we headed for the giant Ngorongoro Crater.

As we reached the outer slopes of the crater, the farmland made way for thick high altitude forest, for even at its base, Ngorongoro is over fifteen hundred metres above sea level, rising to about three thousand metres at its rim. We followed the steep track winding its way through the forest and leading to the rim. Soon we entered clouds and saw the mist swirl among the 'old man's beard' lichen hanging from the ghostly shapes of gnarled trees. We briefly glimpsed a leopard sneaking through thick bushes and a bushbuck tiptoeing among the trees until it disappeared in the mist. Here and there in the forest were small open glades where we saw the dark shapes of buffalo grazing silently.

Ngorongoro Crater is what remains of a volcano which last erupted about two million years ago. It must have reached thousands of metres higher into the sky than its three thousand metres of today, for after its final eruption, its cone collapsed inwards to form the existing caldera, the crater floor a thousand metres below the rim, fifteen kilometres across and 250 square kilometres in area. We soon reached the rim of the crater and saw the spectacular scenery below us. The bottom of the crater consists mainly of grassland but it also contains a little forest of yellow fever trees and a small lake where up to a million pink flamingoes feed. At first sight, the country far below us looked empty, but as we stared harder and looked through binoculars, we could see that what looked like tiny specks were really thousands of animals.

I have lived in the crater for a number of years and would have liked to revisit it on this trip but, with the fresh supplies we had bought, it was important to get them stored in my camp on the Serengeti as soon as possible. We drove on for many kilometres along the crater rim until, on the other side and many thousands of metres below, we could see the vast Serengeti plains, stretching as far as the horizon. We put the cars into four wheel drive and slowly descended the steep outer slope of the Ngorongoro Crater. An hour later we drove on to the open plains.

3. The Plains

The vast open plains and acacia tree country are the landscapes I like most. In the forests we had only occasionally seen a lone antelope or, with luck, a pair with an offspring. On the plains we could see herds of wildebeests, zebras, Thomson gazelles, Grant's gazelles and many others.

Herds can exist on the plains because large quantities of their food, grass, grow close together: in the forest individual food plants are often widely spread out. Grasses evolved to withstand grazing and are in fact highly advanced plants in many ways. In addition to having small flowers which rely on the wind for pollination, they have tough stems which run horizontally along the ground or just under it. This means that when herbivores graze off the tops or fires sweep the grasslands, the roots and stems remain undamaged and the foliage grows again quickly. Furthermore grazing and, to a certain extent, fires encourage the development of grasslands, removing woody plants and old vegetation which would otherwise grow up and displace many grass species.

Until about fifty million years ago Africa had no extensive open plains, nor any mountains; instead the continent consisted of a gentle undulating landscape with vast tropical forests. At that time the temperature throughout much of the world was tropical: London, Paris and New York had the same climate as Malaysia has today and dense humid forests in which sabre-toothed tigers roamed covered the USA and much of Europe. Subsequently, the global temperature dropped and in many areas of the northern hemisphere the tropical forests were replaced by coniferous forests which were better able to cope with the colder weather. It was also drier and this made many areas unsuitable for the growth of forests. This meant that the grasses had an opportunity to expand, and as a result, enormous open plains evolved in America and in Africa.

The spread of grasses over large areas of East Africa may well have been helped further by the birth of the Great Rift Valley, the huge fault in the earth's crust which is a continuation of the original drifting apart of the continents, and will ultimately separate East Africa from the rest of Africa. When the Great Rift Valley came into being it in turn gave birth to numerous volcanoes. When they erupted, they undoubtedly caused extensive fires which exterminated large areas of forest.

As the tropical forests became smaller and the grasslands larger, many herbivores began occasionally to venture out of the forests in search of food and adapt to a life on the open plains. The process of moving out of the forest and living full time in open country, with its new dangers, was presumably a slow one.

OPPOSITE: Topi often stand on termite mounds from where they have a better view to spot any predator. In the forest bushbuck use the same protective system.

OVERLEAF (pp. 108–9): Buffalo herds may contain many hundreds of animals. Although lions do prey on buffalo, usually lone individuals or those in smaller herds, a buffalo may charge at lions, even when unprovoked.

OVERLEAF (pp. 110–1 TOP): When the rainy season starts, many of the herbivores, including zebras, migrate away from bush and tall grass, where it is more difficult to spot predators, and on to the short grass plains where succulent grass and enough waterholes will be available.

OVERLEAF (pp. 110–1 BOTTOM): Packs of African wild dogs, consisting of related males which have been joined by one or more adult females originating in another pack, usually hunt during the coolness of dusk or dawn.

OVERLEAF (pp. 112–3 TOP): Although leopards usually hunt at night it is not uncommon for them to seek prey in daytime, often during the heat of mid-day when many of the gazelles are moving about less.

OVERLEAF (pp. 112–3 BOTTOM): Two lions of the same pride fight briefly because of a lioness in oestrus. Up to six adult males, usually brothers, may co-operate to take over one or two prides of females from the resident males.

The behaviour of Bohor reedbuck demonstrates how the early antelopes may have behaved when starting to move out into open country. Although Bohor reedbuck are normally solitary creatures or live in family units of a male with one or two females, they often associate in groups of up to a hundred individuals when moving out of the reeds and feeding in the open. The advantage of large groups is that more eyes are available to look out for danger. Yet when lying down to rest in the open, reedbuck divide into slightly separated groups, the family units. Although Bohor reedbuck display the beginnings of herd behaviour, they still retain strong remnants of the behaviour of their forest ancestors: if danger threatens, each individual creeps away separately into the reed vegetation to hide, lying absolutely still. In this way their behaviour is no different from that of the forest duikers.

The first herbivores moving on to the open plains must have fed in a similar way near the edge of the forest, disappearing back into the forest whenever danger threatened. As they ventured further and further on to the open plains, however, it became difficult to reach the safety of the forest. In fact, because a predator was most likely to emerge from the forest, the plains herbivores started to run away from cover. This is one of the basic differences in behaviour between forest and open country herbivores.

After driving across the plains for two hours we reached a patch of acacia tree country around Lake Ndutu and were soon approaching camp, where I could see Maro chopping firewood while Paulo was sweeping the groundsheet of one of the tents. They stopped their work to greet us. We unpacked the cars and then relaxed for a while, catching up on the news. Nothing much unusual had happened during our absence. The wild genet cat had given birth to four kittens in the store. An elephant had been into camp and had threatened to push down one of the trees, but Maro had persuaded it to change its mind by shouting at it. The lions had regularly wandered among the tents at night and had roared a lot and a hyaena had stolen a pan which had subsequently been found mangled among the bushes. It was great to be home again.

It often amuses me to have friends visit me because although I have told them that animals wander through the camp, it seems to be almost impossible for someone from Europe or the USA to take this too seriously. I think they think I am exaggerating a bit. I remember one couple visiting me. During supper the surrounding landscape was quiet but for the chirping of crickets. When it came time to bid them goodnight, I said to the couple,

'I have parked the car behind your tent. In the very unlikely event that a lion should be a nuisance, just unzip the flap at the back of the tent and you are one step away from the car.'

They looked at me for a while and then one of them said,

'You are joking, aren't you? Surely no lions come here?'

Feeling rather guilty, although I don't know why, I explained that they did move through camp quite regularly. That night, however, all was peaceful. In spite of this I am afraid that my friends arrived for breakfast looking bleary-eyed, having apparently not slept very well.

When we returned from Dar es Salaam, life soon settled back into its usual pattern. While Sirili, Maro and Paulo took care of the camp, and Renatus and Lawrence serviced the vehicles and other mechanical devices such as the generator for charging batteries and the chain saw for cutting firewood, I went out daily to film and photograph animals.

On one such trip I came across a troop of banded mongooses and it occurred to me that the first predators to leave the forest and start living on the open plains were probably the small species such as mongooses which can hide in grass. Of course, many of the large predators soon wandered further out into open country to hunt too. Their prey, unable to hide, had to rely on speed to escape and so the open plains herbivores developed longer legs with which they could run faster. At the same time they developed keener eyesight so that they could spot danger from a distance.

Running is all very well for adult herbivores but how about new born and young animals? Almost as soon as, for instance, a Thomson gazelle fawn is born, it tries to stand but, for the first few minutes, it will keep toppling over, falling on to its nose, bottom or side. Within four minutes it can stand and even walk towards its mother. I have watched a mother back away for a while as if forcing the fawn to walk more. Finally, the fawn reached its mother and, after nosing about a bit between her forelegs and along her body, found what it was looking for. It suckled for the first time and then lay flat in the grass, looking, except from very close by, like a small bare patch of earth. Its mother moved away about thirty metres and started to graze. I knew she would return regularly throughout the day to feed the youngster. The fawns' reliance on camouflage and hiding is a pattern of behaviour inherited from their forest ancestors. This is possible in open country because they are small and do not move about much in search of food. In fact antelope calves and gazelle fawns are most at risk when they need to stand up and feed, and so are fully visible. Gazelle fawns develop quickly, though, and can run quite fast by the time they are a week old. The danger period is therefore kept to a minimum.

One of the gazelle fawns' major predators is the golden jackal. Golden jackals live in pairs, but when hunting for insects or rodents, each one of the pair will hunt on its own. Interestingly, they will stay together when hunting gazelle fawns, apparently deciding beforehand what prey they are going to hunt. I have no idea how they communicate this decision to each other. In searching for gazelle fawns, the two jackals will thoroughly inspect any longer patches of vegetation where the fawns may be lying hidden and motionless. Of course, some predators can use their sense of smell to try and locate a prey, but antelope calves appear to be odourless. They also do not produce urine or faeces, which could attract predators, until they are licked by the mother, who eats the waste.

OVERLEAF: Thomson gazelles, able to run at 70 kph, rely on speed and distance to outrun a pursuing predator, in this case a lioness. Forest antelopes are more likely to run a short distance and then hide, an option not normally available to herbivores in open country.

TOP: A Wildebeest mother unsuccessfully tries to defend her calf from a spotted hyaena, which contrary to popular belief, is not a cowardly scavenger but a powerful predator.

BOTTOM: Cheetahs, the fastest mammals on earth and able to run at 110 kph, sometimes do not kill a captured gazelle fawn but present it live to their cubs so that the youngsters can practise hunting.

OVERLEAF: Small rhino calves are a favourite prey of spotted hyaenas. Although a mother rhino tries to protect her calf she is usually too cumbersome to catch the faster predator.

Thus a hunting pair of jackals must find a gazelle by sight. By the time they get close enough, the gazelle fawn will have seen them and will jump up and run away.

In running away a Thomson gazelle fawn will often change direction erratically and then suddenly lie down and remain motionless, as the duiker does in the forest. However, unlike the duiker, which can zigzag among trees and bushes, the gazelle fawn does not have such vegetation to obscure it from view; normally the predator will see where it tries to hide. During the chase, the mother gazelle will often make it difficult for the predator to concentrate on the fawn by zigzagging in front of it. This zigzagging behaviour is inherited from the forest ancestors but is used here in a new way. In addition, if the predator is small enough, say no larger than a jackal, the mother gazelle may actually chase it and try to attack. Jackals have learnt to cope with this distraction behaviour. While the mother gazelle distracts one of the pair, the other will often manage to concentrate on the fawn.

I remember once following a lone golden jackal hunting for insects. A mother gazelle watched anxiously. She obviously had a fawn hidden in the area. Suddenly a small shape jumped up in front of the jackal, which immediately pursued it. The mother gazelle charged desperately after the jackal and had almost caught up with it when suddenly she stopped and stared. A moment later so did the jackal. And so did I. We had all been fooled. It was not a gazelle fawn running ahead of them but a speedy hare!

On the Serengeti and in the Ngorongoro Crater all three species of African jackal occur: the golden or Asiatic jackal; the side-striped; and the silver-back jackal, also called black-backed or saddle-backed. Few people who have not actually watched jackals in detail can tell the species apart accurately. This is because the thickness and colouring of each jackal's coat changes throughout the year and can resemble that of another species. Golden jackals may have a darker saddle and so be confused with the saddle-backed jackal. Individual saddle-backed jackals may have a white tip to their tail rather than the more normal black tip and thus be confused with the side-striped jackal which normally has a white-tipped tail. To add to all this, side-striped jackals may not always have a white stripe on their sides and so can be confused with golden jackals!

Members of all three species live in pairs. Normally once a year the female gives birth to about four offspring. Previous offspring may remain with the parents to help look after the next litter so that a family often consists of ten members and occasionally more.

Until about fifteen years ago it was not thought that jackals would tackle anything larger than a young gazelle. Then one day I was on the short grass plains of the Serengeti and looking through my binoculars I thought I could see two golden jackals chasing an adult Thomson gazelle. I could only see shimmering forms in the heat haze and could not be sure I was making an accurate observation. The three forms disappeared over the crest of a hill. I was excited because if I could confirm my observation, it would be new information. I spent some time carefully checking the exact spot I would have to head for in this almost featureless landscape and then drove as fast as I could. As I came over the crest of the small hill, sure enough there were two jackals eating a fully adult gazelle. I subsequently spent many weeks following golden jackals on the Serengeti plains and saw them hunt adult gazelles on quite a few occasions. Although when hunting adult gazelles jackals normally move around in pairs or together with the sub adults in family packs, I have occasionally seen a lone jackal successfully tackle an adult gazelle.

It was also thought that the serval cat, about twice the size of a domestic cat but spotted like a leopard, only hunted fairly small creatures, although I had seen one in a forest with a captured Sykes monkey. Then one day I discovered a serval cat with a dead adult Thomson gazelle. The shy cat ran away and I found that the Thomson gazelle was still warm and had the serval's tooth marks in its throat.

Serval cats have very large ears, an indication that they hunt a lot by sound. I used to follow a serval cat and often watched fascinated as it listened carefully for the rustling of rodents. It apparently pinpointed the exact position of the prey before pouncing over the long grass. In landing the serval spread its front paws wide around its prey and then quickly scooped the rodent towards its mouth, killing it with a bite.

Servals are not the only creatures which can hunt by sound alone. Jackals sometimes do but bat-eared foxes are the extreme example: they can locate insects feeding underground and know exactly where to dig for them.

I once watched some young bat-eared foxes playfully approach an adult male Thomson gazelle. Much to my surprise, the gazelle joined in the game, bucking and chasing the young foxes in circles. The amazing speed with which the bat-eared foxes zigzagged back and forth was a delight to watch and would undoubtedly make it almost impossible for any large predator to capture one of these creatures. The Thomson gazelle left when a golden jackal approached and the young foxes disappeared into their den, but the two adult foxes confronted the jackal, arching their backs and tails just like a cat. The jackal retreated, avoiding a showdown, and soon disappeared from sight. The bat-eared foxes curled up and went to sleep, just as humans may react to tension by going to sleep as if trying to close out their problems.

The Serengeti contains one of the greatest spectacles on earth, the wildebeest migration which involves some two million animals. They congregate on the short grass plains around my camp every rainy season. Although I have seen this phenomenon every year over the past two decades, it still fills me with amazement to see the landscape covered with animals from one horizon to the other. This year was no different and I would often drive through vast herds.

TOP: Spotted hyaenas in the Ngorongoro Crater often successfully hunt flamingoes which need to run over water first before being able to take to the air.

BOTTOM: Cheetahs may tackle large prey such as adult wildebeests and zebras which are about four times their own weight.

Many of the wildebeests had small calves and on one of my excursions I saw a female who had just given birth. The new born calf was desperately trying to stand up but kept losing its balance and tumbling over. Within a few minutes, however, it was standing and walked unsteadily towards its mother. After some searching it began to suckle. When it had finished the mother walked away and her calf followed her, walking quite well now. While new born hartebeest and eland calves lie down to hide, as the Thomson gazelles do, wildebeest calves, by being able to follow their mother immediately, seem to have taken evolution a stage further. However they are very vulnerable for the first week or so when they are unable to outrun predators. As a protective device the calf walks next to its mother, almost touching her side, and the mother places herself between her calf and the predator. This may not sound a very effective defence but in fact it is surprising how difficult it often is to see the calf. In spite of this a great many calves become prey. To ensure that most survive, the wildebeest females nearly all give birth within a three week period. As a result the predators suddenly have an over-abundance of easy prey. They soon become satiated and are unable to eat more.

By the time they are two weeks old the wildebeest calves are able to run almost as fast as their mothers and so the greatest danger period is past. Of course, like other herbivores on the open plains, wildebeests are protected further by living in herds. This is sometimes so effective that it is not uncommon to see almost starving lions among the migration, unable to creep up on any wildebeests without being seen. In fact as far as lions are concerned their hunting success is often greater when there are fewer animals around. This can also depend on other circumstances. I remember that one night there was a tremendous thunderstorm. Under the cover of darkness, with the thunder drowning any other sounds, the lions had a real killing orgy: I found three lions next morning with thirty dead wildebeests lying around them, far more than they could eat. During another similar night on the Serengeti, a pack of hyaenas killed four hundred Thomson gazelles in an area of about one hundred square metres. It is similar to a fox getting into a chicken run and going haywire as it suddenly finds easy prey.

Although lions, and also leopards, may have great difficulty in hunting among large herds, this is much less true for hyaenas and wild dogs, both long distance runners. The tough hyaenas especially thrive among the large herds, perhaps because they can run and hunt effectively on dark nights. The wild dogs, whose slender legs make them more vulnerable to injury, normally hunt at dawn and dusk and on moonlit nights. They have an interesting method of approaching prey. The pack walk closely bunched together with their heads held low and move forward almost hesitantly, some or all occasionally stopping before proceeding again. From a distance this makes them look like a herd of grazing animals and in this manner the wild dogs can get quite close before their intended prey starts to flee and needs to be chased. However if wild dogs

stay in one small area for a long time, then it is noticeable that the temporarily resident herds are on the 'look out' for them and start fleeing at a much greater distance, making hunting far more difficult and often unsuccessful. Undoubtedly to counter this, the wild dogs are semi-nomadic, moving fifteen to twenty kilometres per day and covering an area of about 4000 square kilometres per month.

African wild dogs, also called hunting dogs or Cape hunting dogs, are not domestic dogs which have gone wild. They could have been called African wolves except that wolves are much more closely related to domestic dogs than are the African wild dogs. In the course of evolution the dog family has started to lose one of its toes, the remnant being represented by the dew claw some way up the side of the foot. The dew claw can be a hazard for running dogs since if its legs come too close together the dew claw can get caught and cut the opposite leg or be damaged itself. It is not uncommon for owners of racing greyhounds to have the dew claw amputated. The African wild dogs, however, during their evolution have lost the dew claw entirely.

When I started studying wild dogs, for a book about predators, I was not looking forward to it. Little to nothing was known about their behaviour but from what I had read and from my own limited observations it seemed that their behaviour was very stylised with little variety. I soon found that this was far from the truth. Their social organisation and behaviour is both complex and fascinating.

A wild dog pack can range in size from a couple of individuals to sixty or more. The average size is about ten although fifteen to twenty animals in a pack are not uncommon. Almost invariably there are more males than females in a pack and over a period of time I discovered that the males in a pack are all related. While the females in a pack are also likely to be related to each other, they will have originated from another pack. For instance on one occasion six sisters left the pack of their birth and found a male pack which they joined. Normally unrelated wild dogs are aggressive to one another and so in order to be accepted into the male pack, these females came into a false heat to make themselves sexually attractive. This false heat lasted many weeks, by which time they had been integrated into the pack.

Within the pack there are two separate dominance hierarchies, that of the males and that of the females. It is extremely rare for an individual of one sex to get involved in squabbles related to the dominance hierarchy of the opposite sex. Yet something like pair bonds develop between members of the opposite sex. The major pair bond is between the dominant male and the dominant female. Should the dominant male lose his status to one of the other males then the dominant female immediately transfers her allegiance to the new dominant male. A change in the dominance hierarchy among the males is quite common and in fact in the Genghis pack, the pack I studied in most detail, almost every male was dominant at one time or another. It would be interesting to know if this is also true for other packs, for one would not normally expect the most subordinate male in a group ever to become dominant.

In females the dominance hierarchy is more stable, although changes do sometimes occur. Once a female group has joined a male pack, then over the next few years the dominant female will try to expel all other females from the pack. There are good reasons for this, which are related to the nomadic lifestyle of the wild dogs. When a female wild dog is due to give birth, she selects an existing den, which may originally have been dug out by an aardvark, decades before, and may subsequently have been inhabited by a succession of other creatures. The den is selected by the pregnant female about three to four weeks before the birth of her pups and during that time she regularly visits the den, cleans it out and makes sure no other creatures take up residence. To force the pack to give up their nomadic lifestyle and remain with her, she comes into a false heat. Once she has given birth, the males are so attracted to the pups that it is not necessary for the mother to continue her false heat. The pups depend solely on the mother's milk for three weeks and subsequently eat meat which is regurgitated to them by the adult dogs returning from a hunt. At three months old the pups leave the den for good and start their nomadic life with the adults.

If a pack contains more than one female each may give birth at different times and the nomadic lifestyle of the dogs may be interrupted frequently, especially if females give birth within some weeks of each other. As a result there are more pups to feed, usually about ten per mother. At the same time, because the dogs have to hunt for many months in a fairly small area, usually a thirty kilometre radius around the den, it is very noticeable that the prey learn to expect the dogs and flee at a far greater distance. So just when hunting success should increase in order to feed the larger number of pups, in addition to the adults, the opposite happens. The survival of the whole pack is put at risk. The dominant female, by expelling the subordinate females from the pack, makes this less probable and so increases the chances of survival of her own offspring.

It may take years for the dominant female to accomplish her task, because something has to spark off this behaviour: she only starts to expel a subordinate female when the latter comes into heat. As a result, the subordinate female leaves but is accompanied by the male she formed a bond with. These two mate over a period of three days while separated from the pack. Subsequently they may try to join the pack again; if successful, the subordinate female will give birth to her pups within the pack and therefore the dominant female will not have accomplished her task. Not only that but the attraction of pups is so great that normally the dominant female will actively help to look after the subordinate female's pups and may even temporarily steal them and treat them as her own. Only on one occasion have I seen a dominant female kill the pups

LEFT: Like most predators, lions will scavenge and are often attracted to a carcass by seeing vultures landing.

BELOW: Young lions, having caught a buffalo calf, are apparently too inexperienced to know how to kill their prey efficiently by applying a bite to the throat as adult lions normally do.

TOP: Although a family of jackals may co-operate during a hunt, they are often aggressive during feeding, the subordinate quickly making a submissive gesture to the dominant individual.

BOTTOM: It is a nasty sight seeing spotted hyaenas, like most dog-like creatures, kill their prey by eating. However, death usually occurs as quickly as when a lion or leopard applies the throat bite.

of a subordinate one and this was when hunting had become extremely difficult and the difference in size between her own pups and those of the subordinate female's was considerable, so that there could be no confusion as to which pups belonged to whom. Even so, she did not kill the last one, which I named Solo, but instead put it with her own pups. Maybe, because it was closer in size to her own pups, she thought it was one of her own.

A subordinate female, after being in heat, will not always return to the pack. In this case her mate remains with her and helps to look after the litter born about 73 days later. I have never been able to ascertain what ultimately becomes of the subordinate female and her litter but suspect that they try and avoid their original pack and in so doing leave its 4000 square kilometre territory. The male, however, returns to his original pack when his offspring are about seven months old: an extremely strong bond exists between male siblings and lasts for life.

The male sibling bond is interesting to watch within a pack which consists of various generations of male offspring. In any conflict between an older and younger dog, siblings always support each other. Furthermore, when a pack is resting, one may often see separate groups of dogs lying together. More often than not these groups are composed of siblings.

Sometimes a cold wind blows over the plains and the dogs can help to keep each other warm by lying in a group, all closely huddled together. Of course the dog on the windward side is in the worst position and I watched amused one day when every minute or so the dog on that side would move to the leeward side of the pile. As a result over the next few hours the whole pile of dogs was slowly progressing so that they ended up resting in a totally different place from where they had started.

Dogs hunt when it is cool. This can be at dawn, dusk, during moonlit nights or after a rain storm. It used to be said that the African wild dogs hunt in relays, some starting the hunt in front but others taking over when the front dogs become tired. This statement was based on inaccurate observations. I almost invariably found that the fastest runners would try to stay in front. Sometimes, however, when the prey zigzagged or ran in a large circle, less fast dogs could cut corners and end up in front. It was also said that once a pack of wild dogs had selected a prey, the chosen victim had no chance of escape because the dogs would pursue it for many kilometres until the prey was exhausted. This is not correct. Wild dogs may pursue their prey for as much as five or six kilometres and then give up. In fact of the hundreds of hunts I have watched, fifty per cent of the intended prey escaped.

Thomson and Grant's gazelles have a way of escaping their predators which, at first glance, almost seems like play. It is a gait called 'stotting' whereby the gazelle leaps forward, lands with stiff legs, and bounds forward again. There has been considerable puzzlement among scientists as to why they should do this. One theory held that it was a sort of alarm signal to other gazelles. I have come to the conclusion, however, that it is a system of running which utilises less energy. I once watched a Grant's gazelle being chased by wild dogs and stotting in large jumps away in front of them. Whenever a dog got too close, the gazelle would change to normal running, increase the distance between itself and the predators and then stot again. It kept this up for over five kilometres, one of the longest chases I have seen, and finally the dogs gave up, obviously realising they had little chance of catching the gazelle.

A pack of dogs must co-operate closely if they are to be successful in tackling large prey such as zebras. Since zebras live in family groups, led by a stallion, and such families may join up into very large herds when pursued, the dogs must first try to separate one individual. In trying to do this they are continually harassed by the stallions which may zigzag in front of the dogs, occasionally kicking at them or turning to bite. However, once an individual zebra has been separated from the herd, the front dog tries to grab its tail and when it has got hold of it, digs in its heels, thus slowing the zebra down. The next dog then tries to grab the zebra's upper lip. If this is successful, it is almost impossible for the zebra to move: this tactic is similar to the twitch used by man on horses, holding its upper lip when force-feeding medicine to it. Once the first two dogs have more or less immobilised the zebra, the rest of the pack can move in for the kill.

The hunting of zebras by wild dogs is not common, at least on the Serengeti. In fact it appears that some packs never hunt zebras while in others it may have become a custom and, fascinatingly, may depend on one or two dogs. In the Genghis pack it was only the two largest dogs, Yellow Peril and Genghis, who could completely immobilise a zebra by holding on to its lip. When these two older males died, the pack hunted zebras less frequently and ten years later only two dogs in the pack, which had decreased in size to five adult members, had ever been involved in hunting zebras. Then something interesting happened. These two dogs captured a zebra, one holding on to the tail and the other on to the upper lip. But the other three dogs did not move in for the kill. They just watched from a distance, apparently not knowing what to do. So the two older dogs had to let their prey go. The custom was obviously disappearing from the Genghis pack.

The relationships within a family herd of zebras are very close indeed. I once watched wild dogs chase some zebras and manage to isolate a mare with her foal and a yearling which, I guessed, was the mare's elder offspring. I don't know whether the other zebras did not notice this, but in any case they ran off, disappearing from sight. Left on their own, the mare and her two offspring stopped, bunched so close together that their sides touched. Four of the dogs approached them but the mother zebra moved forward trying to bite one of the dogs. As she did so, the other three dogs tried to grab the foal from behind but were headed off by the yearling which lunged forward in the foal's defence. Time and again the dogs tried to get at the foal but were always headed off by

OVERLEAF: A lion sniffs the air and pulls a flemen face after being passed by a lioness coming into oestrus.

137

the mare or the yearling. But neither of the zebras took more than a few steps away from the foal, which was able to maintain its position, pressed to its mother's side.

As the minutes went by, however, the dogs became bolder and I didn't think the mare and her yearling would be able to defend the foal much longer. Then suddenly I felt the ground vibrating and, looking around, I saw ten zebras fast approaching. Soon afterwards the herd closed its ranks around the mother and her two offspring and then the closely packed group galloped away. The dogs chased them for about fifty metres but were unable to penetrate the herd and soon gave up.

The ancestor of the zebras and horses, called the 'dawn horse', was a small, hare-like animal which had slender limbs and probably lived in forests and swamps. It had four toes on its front feet and three toes on its hind feet. It and some of its descendants were browsers, feeding on leaves rather than grass, but as they adapted to grasslands they became grazers and as with most open country species they increased their speed by evolving longer legs. As they evolved over millions of years they lost their side toes, until they were running on their elongated middle toes whose nails had thickened to form protective, shock-absorbent hooves. Other changes also occurred: their rounded teeth, suited to forest browsing, could not cope with the hard silica which occurs in grasses and so they evolved bigger molars with hard ridges of dentine on them. Another problem facing a grazer is the head down position which makes it difficult to detect predators while feeding; the higher up the eyes are, the better. Together with the necessity of providing space for the enlarged molars, this resulted in an elongation of the skull.

From North America, the horse's ancestors migrated into Eurasia and on into Africa, where some evolved into donkeys and zebras. In North America itself, for some unknown reason, horses became extinct. They were re-introduced by the Spanish conquistadors, about 300 years ago.

In Africa zebras were the successful species, their most distinctive characteristic being the black and white stripes. To some extent these stripes may serve as a camouflage in bush country but most zebras in fact live in grassland and are very visible from long distances. What purpose do the stripes serve, then? It seems to me that there are two possible functions. At night, in moonlight, zebras are almost invisible except at very close quarters and so this is an effective camouflage. Equally important, when a predator chases a prey, it normally picks out one individual, probably one it thinks is weaker, and chases that. However, trying to concentrate on a particular striped body bouncing up and down among many others must be quite confusing. When pursued over a distance by wild dogs or hyaenas, zebras increase this confusion even more by numerous families bunching up while fleeing, sometimes into herds of many hundreds. Zebra stallions will create further diversions by zigzagging in front of the predators and at times even attack them with bites and kicks.

OPPOSITE: Zebra foals learn to stand and walk within minutes of birth.

141

OPPOSITE TOP: The Maasai tribe have traditionally tolerated wild animals. However, contrary to popular belief, they do occasionally eat wild animals and do not survive solely on the milk and blood from their cattle.

OPPOSITE BOTTOM: Most predators, including hyaenas, become more lively when it is cooler after sunset and in fact at times almost seem to change character, becoming far bolder and therefore potentially more dangerous.

When a herd is resting at night each adult takes turns in standing sentry duty. Even youngsters take their turn but, perhaps because they are inexperienced, the adults only let them do so for short periods.

The stripes on a zebra are different in each individual just as fingerprints are in humans. Yet to some extent the general characteristics of the stripes may be inherited. For instance a mother with wide stripes may pass this on to her offspring and such slight variations may occur within the whole family herd. Quite often on the Serengeti I have seen individuals which have a white saddle of hair on their backs and in other areas spotted zebras occasionally occur. Judging from the fossil records not all new species evolve slowly; some may evolve suddenly over a short period. It is thought that this may happen when a relatively small number of a certain species is isolated from others of its kind (say in a small forest surrounded by open plains) and inbreeding occurs. Thus if zebras with the gene which produces spots were isolated, then soon all individuals within that area would have spots. This is of course no different from the way in which man has bred many breeds of domestic animals. The big difference is that in the wild the changes must also help protect the animal from predators, or at least not be an obstruction to escaping them.

It has often been claimed that an albino animal has less chance of survival because it will be more easily seen by its predators. I don't believe this is completely true, because I have seen predators refrain from attacking an unusual looking individual. In other words, as long as albinos are very uncommon, they have a good chance of surviving. If predators become accustomed to seeing them, they will not hesitate to hunt them. In that case albinos, being more visible, are certainly at a disadvantage.

As well as being wary of strange looking members of familiar prey species, predators may also react cautiously to species they have apparently never seen before.

Once, when I was watching the Genghis pack of wild dogs resting, they suddenly all jumped up and stared. Among the passing zebra migration were a number of donkeys. They had obviously joined the migration when it passed a Maasai village. I held my breath. The donkeys had probably never encountered a predator before without the protection of their Maasai herdsman and so might not run off if approached by the dogs. Even if they did, donkeys are not fast runners and would have no chance at all of outrunning the dogs. However, nothing happened. The dogs just stood and stared as if trying to work out whether these were strange zebras or some new weird animal which might be dangerous. A few days later I met a Maasai searching for the donkeys but by then the zebra migration had moved far into the park and I don't know whether he ever found them again.

I remember another time seeing a wild cat with white and ginger coloured patches in its coat, probably resulting from its mother having interbred with a domestic cat. It was being followed closely by a number of inquisitive

OPPOSITE: Zebra stallions sometimes fight for the possession of a harem which consists of up to ten mares. Zebra families may join up to form very large herds as a protection against pursuing hyaenas or wild dogs, the stallions protecting the rear by biting and kicking.

Thomson gazelles which had apparently never seen such a strange creature before. The cat did not seem to like being followed because the tip of its tail twitched back and forth and occasionally it turned and charged the very much larger gazelles.

On another occasion a friend of mine, James Malcolm, who at the time was helping me with the wild dog studies, saw a bushpig on the plains, at least eighty kilometres away from its normal forest or thick bush habitat. The Genghis pack were accustomed to warthogs, which are common on the plains and which they would normally attack. But they did no more than stare in apparent amazement at this strange hog-like creature with long hair.

The reactions of the dogs may give a clue as to how a species can travel successfully through an unusual habitat and colonise a new one. Maybe occasionally a small group of, say, bushpigs travels across the short grass plains, possibly because of over-population in their original habitat, and finally reaches a riverine forest on the other side of the Serengeti where no bushpigs occur. They could settle there and start a new colony. It is in fact not uncommon for species to occur where one would not expect them. I have seen a blue monkey west of Lake Ndutu which is at least sixty kilometres from its usual forest habitat.

Another interesting creature which must have travelled at least forty kilometres across the plains is a lone crocodile which lives in Lake Masak, next to Lake Ndutu. I imagine it crept across the plains during the rainy season when the ground was wet and muddy in many places.

Some familiar prey animals, instead of looking strange to their predators, may surprise them by acting strangely. One such incident involved a large Kori bustard. It suddenly appeared from among some low sodom apple plants close to the Genghis pack of wild dogs. The bird was obviously wounded, for it dragged one wing and was unsteady on its feet, swaying from side to side as it ran away. The dogs immediately pursued it and had little trouble in catching up. At the last moment and apparently with great effort the bird ran a bit faster and flew for about ten metres before landing again and hobbling off. The dogs soon caught up. Again the bird took to the air with great effort but once more only managed a short distance. When the dogs were almost on top of the bird, it suddenly stopped staggering about. It ran fast and took to the air with no trouble. It had successfully lured the wild dogs away from its nest. This event was especially fascinating to me because I had previously seen a Kori bustard at her nest react to the approach of a spotted hyaena. In this case however the bustard did not feign injury; to my amazement it fluffed out its feathers and wings and with head held low and beak pointed forward, went straight towards the hyaena. The hyaena stared at this threatening apparition, as if it had never seen anything like it before, and then retreated, slowly at first but a good deal faster when the bird dashed forward.

Spotted hyaenas do occasionally hunt birds. I remember one day following

OPPOSITE TOP: Lions are the most social of the cat family and, within a pride, often like having close physical contact with each other which is established with the aid of friendly gestures.

OPPOSITE BOTTOM: African wild dogs, especially adult and sub-adult females, usually compete in looking after pups, often catching any youngster which wanders too far and carrying it back to the den.

a male hyaena in the Ngorongoro Crater. He led me to the mouth of the Munge River where it flows into the soda lake, so called because of the high concentration of soda salts in the water. There were thousands and thousands of pink flamingoes bathing in the fresh river water, washing off the soda salts as they must do daily if their feathers are not to clog up with salt and render them incapable of flying.

As we arrived the flamingoes retreated slightly into the lake. The hyaena stopped, sniffed the ground and then lay down, closing his eyes. Some way off I could see another hyaena resting. I knew it was a female, for female hyaenas are much larger than the males. I stopped the car some thirty metres from the edge of the lake and waited. With peace having returned, the flamingoes soon crowded into the mouth of the Munge River again, obviously enjoying the sweet, fresh water. The male hyaena slept for a while, then opened his eyes and, without moving, studied the birds. He slowly got up and wandered toward them, giving the appearance of being more interested in smells on the ground.

At first most of the flamingoes took little notice but when the hyaena got closer some started to move away. As if this was a signal the hyaena started to run and on reaching the lake continued on into the water as fast as it could. The birds fled, running first to get up speed before taking to the air. Soon an enormous pink cloud rose from the blue lake but the hyaena continued plunging through the water because some of the birds, crowded as they were, had difficulty taking off. Moments later the hyaena plunged in amongst some birds and quickly caught up with one of them. He opened his mouth to grab the bird. At the same moment, however, the hyaena disappeared in a froth of white foam: he had run into a deep patch and gone under. Soon afterwards, though, he reappeared. As he swam back to shallow water, his head all wet and hair dark and smooth, he looked like a seal, searching for fish. When he reached the shore he looked rather sheepish and he lay down and went to sleep as if trying to pretend nothing had happened.

In the course of the next half hour other flamingoes flew in from more distant parts of the lake and started to bathe. Soon it was as packed as before and once more the hyaena got up and chased into the water. This time it was successful: it caught a flamingo. But as it approached the shore with its prize, the much larger female hyaena wandered over and took it away. Full grown female hyaenas are rarely successful in catching flamingoes themselves, probably because there is too much drag in the water from their large bodies. However, they make up for it by completely dominating the males! While the female ate the flamingo, the male waited, but he must have known that the female would leave no scraps for him: when more of the birds arrived to bathe, he hunted again. Finally, close to sunset, he managed to catch another bird. The female, having finished her meal, had left in the direction of the clan's dens and so the male confidently took his prize to the shore and started to eat it. He had barely started, however, when two golden jackals appeared and joined him, dashing

in and out while grabbing small morsels. The hyaena tried to stop them but the jackals were much too fast for him. Finally, when the hyaena had eaten two-thirds of his meal, one of the jackals nipped his bottom and as the hyaena turned to retaliate, the other jackal grabbed the remains of the flamingo and rushed off with it. The hyaena started to chase it but then gave up, knowing it would be a hopeless task. So he wandered away, his head held low, and whooped mournfully. The jackals on the other hand raised their noses to the sky and howled, warning their cubs that a large predator was in the area.

Hyaenas sometimes manage to capture and eat jackal cubs but normally only when the adult jackals are hunting out of sight of the den. Surprisingly, adult jackals, less than a quarter of the size of a hyaena, can give the much larger predator a rough time. I remember once watching a pair of jackals sleeping. At first they did not notice a spotted hyaena approach their den, which contained four young cubs, but the noise of the large predator starting to dig out the cubs woke them up. The two adult jackals immediately jumped up, rushed over to the hyaena and bit its ankles. The hyaena turned around with a growl, trying to bite the male jackal but merely biting into the air: the jackal had already jumped back. In concentrating on the male jackal, the hyaena had turned its bottom toward the female, who immediately bit its ankle again. The hyaena wheeled around, turning its bottom towards the male jackal who quickly took advantage of the situation. Hyaenas apparently have tender ankles and so to protect them, the hyaena lowered itself into a sitting position, covering its ankles. This did not deter the jackals, who now repeatedly nipped the hyaena's bottom. The hyaena retreated but, in order to keep its ankles covered, had to shuffle along on its bottom. The jackals continued their attacks, one on each side of the hyaena which, in trying to avoid their sharp bites, pirouetted away on its bottom.

Spotted hyaenas live in clans consisting of up to a hundred members. Each adult member may wander around on its own within the clan's territory. Should an individual wander across the border, it risks being caught and killed by neighbouring clan members. Thus the borders are marked regularly by border patrols of both clans, each member depositing some scent from a gland on prominent pieces of vegetation. When a female hyaena gives birth, almost always to two cubs, she may do this in a lone den. Subsequently she is likely to carry the cubs to a central den area where most if not all of the females keep their cubs; the youngsters have plenty of playmates and a greater security from predators, especially lions which at times will go out of their way to kill hyaenas, even though they do not eat them. However, adult hyaenas are far from cowardly and I have often seen them tackle lions and chase them away.

During one extraordinary encounter a number of hyaenas confronted three lionesses on a kill. Two of the lionesses left, but the third suddenly ran back, grabbed one of the hyaenas by its neck and shook it vigorously. The other hyaenas immediately attacked the lioness but what surprised me most was that when the lioness let go of her victim, the hyaena, instead of running away, promptly turned and joined in the attack on the lioness, who quickly fled. While spotted hyaenas may stand up to a few lionesses and will occasionally catch and eat lion cubs, they will usually give way to a large pride and to the powerful male lions which are quite a bit bigger than the lionesses.

It used to be believed that hyaenas survived by scavenging off lion kills. In fact hyaenas are highly successful hunters but most of their hunting takes place at night. I have spent many nights following hyaenas. It was exciting and also dangerous work, for I could not use my car lights as this would affect their behaviour. Instead I followed the animals in the moonlight and when they hunted I would have to try and keep up, driving up to 60 kilometres per hour across the dark country and hoping I would see any holes in the dim light.

In the Ngorongoro Crater a clan hunts almost every night and the prey includes animals as large as wildebeests and zebras. While a lone hyaena may chase a Thomson gazelle and even a wildebeest, when hunting zebras they first join up into packs, rather like a jackal family joining up to hunt adult gazelles. The interesting point here is that, like jackals, they apparently can decide beforehand what prey they want. Not only that, but when hyaenas set off in a pack to hunt zebras they normally ignore other potential prey. It seems therefore that they like variety in their diet.

While the members of a clan may co-operate in the chase, there is aggressive competition during feeding. In fact the hyaenas are so closely packed around the kill that many can only get a share by walking and running over the others' backs and literally diving into the mêlée. It is also extremely noisy as individuals whoop and growl and roar and scream.

Sometimes during the chase hyaenas pursue their intended prey across the border of their territory and make the kill within the territory of the neighbouring clan. The noise soon attracts the neighbours from all directions and once their numbers have built up, they charge. The intruders invariably retreat but this seems to encourage the neighbours to pursue them and in doing so they in turn cross the border. Almost immediately the roles are reversed and the new trespassers are chased back across the border again. Sometimes this chasing back and forth may last as long as twenty minutes or so.

The borders are not in fact absolutely permanent. I remember over a period of a year seeing one clan expand its territory on its northern border, but while it concentrated on its battles with those neighbours, it neglected its southern border and lost territory there to another clan. During that year more hyaenas died from fights with other hyaenas than from any other cause and I suspect that there was an over-population of hyaenas in the crater. Today the numbers are far lower and I have not seen any big border fights for a long time now.

Hyaenas are large creatures. One female, killed during a border fight, weighed 85 kilograms. I had to be careful following them at night because I had removed the window next to me to make photography easier, and a fully grown female

was tall enough to stick her head into the landrover without needing to stretch her neck much.

My main potential problem when living in the Ngorongoro Crater was lions. They had almost no fear of humans. At one stage, I used to come back from working nearly every day to find the complete Munge River pride lying in my camp, some of them on the verandah of my dining tent. For the first few days when I drove up to them they would slowly move away thirty metres or so, but soon they got so used to the car arriving that they ignored it. I tried driving straight towards them but they still ignored me. Then I threw a small pebble near them but they only chased it, thinking it a new game. Finally, in desperation, I got out of the car and walked slowly towards them (though without going too far from the car!) and then they calmly got up and moved away a short distance. Later these same lions chased a wildebeest into the camp and killed it next to my bedroom tent. As if that wasn't bad enough, the two large males then started to fight over the meal, chasing each other around the tent and occasionally bumping into the guide ropes so that I was afraid the tent might collapse on top of me. Luckily they finally managed to tear the kill in two and each ate their share on opposite sides of the camp, although with much growling both at each other and at the lionesses and cubs. Needless to say I didn't get much sleep that night.

Normally I am not scared of lions. One night, however, I needed to go to the lavatory which was some thirty metres from my tent. At the time it had been impossible to obtain torch batteries in Tanzania and so I had to make do without a torch. Going there was no problem, but walking back I heard some large feet padding along nearby. There was a lion walking parallel to me. It was a spine-chilling feeling. I knew that if I started running it would encourage the lion to chase me and so I continued walking the next twenty metres at the same speed, as if unconcerned.

I suspect that in prehistoric times the competition between the large predators was fierce. Less than two million years ago there were ancestral tigers and sabre-tooth lions on the Serengeti. It may be that such competition resulted in lions staying in family groups, starting with the female offspring remaining with the mother. Subsequently, when the daughters gave birth, the family would have been extended to include aunts and so prides came into existence. Lions would therefore have been better able to see off other large but more solitary predators. Scientists often seek a single major reason which caused change but of course changes are frequently effected by a combination of factors and so it may have been with lions. Another likely reason for lions starting to live in prides is that this enabled them to tackle larger prey such as buffalo, eland and giraffes. In fact the possible prey animals of the prehistoric lions may well have been larger, for many of the prey animals on the Serengeti went through a period of gigantism. These included buffalo two and a half times their present day size with a horn span of three metres, pigs the size of rhinos

OPPOSITE TOP:
Watched by a Goliath heron, a crocodile grabs for the rotting remains of a creature.

OPPOSITE BOTTOM:
Completely unaware of the approach of a crocodile, this Thomson gazelle finished drinking just in time to avoid being grabbed.

151

TOP: Members of a hyaena clan regularly patrol the borders of their territory, attacking and sometimes killing any intruders they come across.

BOTTOM: Sometimes a hyaena clan will pursue and catch their prey across the clan's border. The sounds made during feeding attract the members of the neighbouring clan and, once sufficient numbers have gathered, they chase the intruders back across the border. In doing so they themselves cross the border and are in turn chased back so that the two clans may chase each other back and forth for fifteen minutes or more.

OVERLEAF TOP LEFT: Impala make enormous jumps, often zigzagging among each other and thereby probably confusing any predator which is trying to concentrate on a single individual.

OVERLEAF BOTTOM LEFT: Waterbuck flee into water when pursued. I suspect they may be protected from crocodiles by possessing distasteful glands in their body.

OVERLEAF RIGHT: By walking on the tips of their hooves which are rubbery, steinbuck can climb almost sheer rocks where even a leopard would have difficulty in following them.

with tusks a metre long, large giraffes with broad moose-like antlers and baboons the size of gorillas.

While within a pride all the females are related, the males, usually brothers, will have originated in another pride, having been expelled when they were about two years old. These young males become nomadic, roaming over a wide area and avoiding resident males. Once they are adult, at the age of about five, they might try to take over a pride from resident males. The battles for possession can result in death and obviously the more brothers there are, the better are their chances of taking over a pride. The number of adult males to a pride can vary from one to six, or even more. I remember watching six brothers grow up in Ngorongoro Crater. When they were adult they were so powerful that they took over two neighbouring prides of females. This did not mean that it became one pride: the lionesses of different prides are antagonistic towards each other. So the prides remained as different entities but the six brothers moved freely between the two. I once saw and heard all six roar at the same time and the ground trembled as if the crater was about to erupt. It was an awe-inspiring experience and I could well imagine other lions staying away from the area. Normally lone nomadic males would have no chance of taking over a pride but they may join up with one or more unrelated nomadic males and form an alliance with them. Once they have taken over a pride, they kill all the young cubs in the pride. As a result the lionesses quickly come into heat, are mated by the new males and so the cubs subsequently born bear the new males' genes. In other words, the new males are not prepared to help raise their predecessors' offspring, only their own. However, lionesses who are pregnant when new males take over a pride manage to fool the males. They quickly come into a false heat and when their cubs are born, the males raise them as their own.

Contrary to popular belief male lions do not rely solely on kills made by the females. They are accomplished hunters themselves and need to be, for they are often on their own as they patrol or visit various parts of their territory. However if they notice the lionesses have made a kill they can be lazy and try to share or more often take over the kill rather than hunt themselves. They may not succeed in this. If the lionesses are in a group and really hungry, they can become extremely aggressive and see a male off. At one time when food had been scarce, I saw four lionesses who had managed to get hold of a kongoni, an antelope of the hartebeest family. The lionesses and the cubs had barely started feeding when the most subordinate of the three males appeared. He rushed up to join the females on the kill but they promptly turned on him. He fled with two lionesses close on his heels, one having dug her claws into the male. The females then returned to the kill and the male merely watched from a distance. Some time later, however, when the lionesses and cubs had eaten quite a bit, the dominant male appeared. When he rushed up to the kill, the females made way. I am not sure whether this was because he was the dominant male or because they had fed and so were less hungry. In any case the male grabbed the remnants and ran off. In the meantime the subordinate male had joined him and the two males squabbled briefly, then fed together.

One often reads of lions co-operating closely during a hunt, some spreading themselves out, while others, usually the males, circle around the intended prey. It is said that when this has been accomplished the males roar, frightening the prey so that they flee straight toward the hidden lionesses. I have never seen this happen. I have seen lions stealthily spread themselves out in a line about fifty metres long when they see a prey animal walking towards them. This increases the chances of the prey approaching one of them closely, or of fleeing away from one lion towards another hidden one. But I have not seen closer co-operation than this.

Sometimes there may be the opposite of co-operation. I shall never forget watching a hungry lioness accompanied by a male, who had apparently eaten recently. The lioness was probably coming into heat because the male did not take his eyes off her and as the hungry lioness repeatedly tried to creep up on gazelles drinking at a waterhole, the male got up, fully visible, to keep her in sight. Sometimes he even walked after her. Needless to say the gazelles couldn't have been warned in a more obvious way.

When lions tackle a large prey, they must normally co-operate in order to bring it down. I remember watching a few lionesses lying together when they noticed an eland. One of the lionesses immediately crept forward stealthily. The eland noticed nothing until the lioness shot out of the high grass. The eland fled but the lioness was already running right alongside, only a metre away. I expected the lioness to jump easily on to the eland. Instead, as she ran along, she looked back and I realised she was waiting for the others to help her tackle the large animal. The other lionesses, however, did not feel like hunting. They just sat and watched. So the chasing lioness finally gave up and the eland bounded away.

Buffalo are an even more formidable prey for lions. I have seen lions catch them and in the Lake Manyara National Park they are the lions' common prey. I once saw a buffalo emerge from bushes and walk straight towards a resting pride of twenty-two lions hidden by the high grass. At first neither the buffalo nor the lions noticed each other. Then suddenly the buffalo saw the lions. Instead of running away, it charged and the surprised cats fled in all directions, one barely escaping the buffalo's horns. It was not the first time I had seen buffalo chase lions but I had certainly never seen twenty-two lions be in such haste to get away from anything.

In areas where sufficient Thomson gazelles, wildebeests, zebras and other smaller prey are available, lions will normally concentrate on those species. This may still not be easy. On the Serengeti only about one hunt in five is successful. In most cases the prey notices the lion before the predator is close enough to run and occasionally a prey may 'fight back' successfully. I remember

OPPOSITE TOP: Golden jackals often chase hyaenas from the vicinity of their den, nipping the larger predator's bottom and more sensitive ankles. As is so often the case the smaller creature, by being quicker and more agile, can dominate the larger one in many situations.

OPPOSITE BOTTOM: Taken by surprise, a buffalo flees from the attack of a black rhino. Subsequently however, when the rhino charged a second time, the buffalo calmly lowered its horns and stood its ground. The rhino veered to the side at the final moment.

one lioness catching up with a zebra and pouncing with its forefeet on to the zebra's rump, digging its claws in. The zebra continued to run and it was an extraordinary sight to see the lioness running along behind on its hindlegs while holding on to the zebra. Then suddenly the zebra kicked back, hitting the lioness in the chest and sending her flying into the air. The lioness lost her grip and the zebra escaped. The lioness then gave up the chase and watched the zebra run off. One would expect that having had such a narrow escape the zebra would run in a panic for a long distance. But this did not happen. When it had increased the distance between itself and the lioness to a hundred metres or less, the zebra stopped and calmly looked back.

Ten years ago I spent many months filming a lion pride which seemed to favour resting among the reeds of a small marsh some kilometres from my camp. This was partly because the dry season had been long and drinking water was scarce, but there were still a few little pools in the marsh. Occasionally an animal would come down to drink but almost invariably they noticed the lions and escaped. This may have been because the resident prey animals had got to know that the lions were likely to be in that area and so were more alert. In any case the large predators faced starvation. They were saved by the small flocks of flamingoes which visited the water pools daily. The lions would sneak through the reeds and then run fast into the water, often capturing one of the birds. There is not much flesh on a flamingo but the lions caught just enough birds every day to survive until the rains brought more animals to the area.

During the dry season the short grass plains become a semi-desert. Yet the resident lion prides manage to survive, usually by concentrating on the few spots which may contain one or two small pools of permanent water and which may attract the few prey animals which have remained in the area. I have got to know a number of these prides and regularly visit them to see how they are managing. One pride almost invariably rests in the shade of some bushes and small trees which grow on top of a kopje situated on the short grass plains about thirty kilometres from my camp. I remember one day watching these lions fast asleep. I then noticed numerous agama lizards approach the lions and without further ado clamber on to the predators. Apart from an occasional twitch the lions took no notice as the lizards ventured over their bodies, catching flies. In fact I suspect the lions were glad to have these small predators relieving them of the bothersome insects.

Not all lions are as used to agama lizards as this pride. I remember once watching a pride resting close together in the shade of an acacia tree. In fact the shade was so sparse that one of the females lay pressed against the tree. Then I noticed an agama lizard climbing head first down the trunk of the tree, catching flies as it went along. Finally it reached the sleeping lioness and, seeing a fly within easy reach on the predator's rump, snapped at it. It missed the fly and instead bit the lioness. The lioness jumped up with a tremendous roar, bringing the whole pride to its feet. She then stared suspiciously at all

the other lions, obviously wondering which one had pinched her bottom.

I spent most of one day with the lions at the kopje but not much happened and so at mid afternoon I left them. There was another pride I wanted to check on before returning to camp. I was pretty sure I would find them: just as the pride I had been watching usually rested on the kopje, their neighbours almost invariably rested next to a tiny lake which is bordered by reeds. The distance was only eight kilometres but the terrain was rough and it took me almost an hour to reach the lake. Actually I suppose it is too small to be called a lake. It is more like a large and permanent waterhole. The lions here have a much easier time during the dry season for it is the only water for many many kilometres and so any animal that needs to drink has little choice but to come here.

I found the pride lying on the green grass not far from the waterhole: three males, four females and numerous cubs of almost a year old. The cubs watched as I arrived. When I stopped the car some of them wandered over and sniffed the vehicle. They knew my car and on occasions they have rested in its shade. Once one of the adult males even tried to push underneath, only half managing it with his great bulk.

When I was watching this pride regularly, I noted with interest that a male Thomson gazelle had established its territory nearby and used to graze calmly less than forty metres from the predators. I never saw the lions attempt to catch it. Perhaps they had tried a number of times when the gazelle first arrived but had given up. I had seen a similar situation near a wild dog den where a number of gazelles resided for many weeks. Although the dogs had to go a long way to hunt, they never tried to catch the gazelles near the den. I can only presume that the gazelles were all healthy individuals which knew where the predators were and could keep a constant eye on them. This made it impossible for the predators to get close enough to have a chance of catching any of the gazelles. The sight of predators and prey living peacefully so close together makes it seem like an Eden, but of course this is a false impression. A mistaken move by the prey can change the scene totally.

Lions are very deceptive. Watching them from a car one feels one could get out and stroke them like a domestic cat, they look so peaceful. Furthermore they seem so lazy that it is almost impossible to imagine how quickly they can react and move. More than one person has been killed because they thought they could stand next to the open door of the car to get a better picture. I respect lions too much to do this, although I was once forced to change a punctured tyre close to a resting pride. The body of the car was between me and the lions and I had a companion keeping an eye on them. All the same, I checked the situation myself every few seconds.

Lions and most of the large cats apparently learn to hunt by observing their mother, but a mother cheetah will teach her cubs by giving them opportunities

OPPOSITE TOP: To discover that Egyptian vultures crack open ostrich eggs by throwing stones at the hard shell was tremendously exciting.

OPPOSITE BOTTOM: Ostriches are one of the last species of large flightless birds left. At one stage in prehistoric times giant flightless birds were the dominant predators but when more powerful predators evolved, the bird's lack of ability to escape by flight resulted in their extermination.

OVERLEAF (pp. 162–3): During the rainy season many cheetahs on the Serengeti may inhabit a territory on the short grass plains, moving back to their dry season territory when the rains come to an end and most prey animals move to more vegetated areas.

OVERLEAF (pp. 164–5): During the rainy season about two million wildebeests congregate on the short grass plains. In spite of having seen this almost every year over the past two decades, I continue to be amazed at the sight of so many herbivores

a young gazelle but sometimes even a wildebeest calf. Very inexperienced cubs will not even be able to kill the prey themselves, and the mother will have to do it for them. On one occasion, I saw a mother allowing her young cubs to creep along with her towards an adult male Thomson gazelle. It was obvious that the gazelle had seen them and that the cheetah mother knew full well that they had no chance of catching it. Invariably during a serious hunt a mother cheetah gives her cubs a soft vocal sign at which the youngsters immediately stop following their mother and wait until she returns to collect them or, having made a kill nearby, calls them to her. During this practice hunt none of these things happened. I watched amused as the three-month-old cubs desperately tried to follow their mother's example. Each time the grazing gazelle started to look up, the mother froze in mid-step. Her cubs were not as quick to react, each freezing at different times and also occasionally having difficulties in maintaining their balance on three legs. To all appearances the gazelle played the game, calmly continuing to graze as if it had seen nothing and then suddenly looking up briefly. More likely, however, the gazelle knew the cheetahs were too far away to be a threat and when they started getting too close, it calmly wandered away a hundred metres and continued to graze.

The social organisation of cheetahs can be confusing. It appears generally that males like to be in small groups, although it is not unusual to see lone ones. The groups of males usually consist of brothers but may occasionally be comprised of males of different ages. Females tend to be more solitary although very rarely sisters may join up for a short while. Of course the females are seldom totally solitary because cubs may remain with their mother until they are about 18 months old. Once the cubs have reached this age, the mother initiates the separation, moving away from them for longer and longer periods. The cubs are now almost fully grown but they often have a very difficult time surviving this period. Although they will have hunted with their mother, they still appear to have much to learn by trial and error. At what stage the sisters are separated from their brothers, I do not know, but I guess within the next six to twelve months.

Presumably sub-adult cheetahs are semi-nomadic but once they are fully grown, they try to establish a sort of territory. I say sort of territory because many other cheetahs may wander through it. However, resident males will chase intruders off. On the Serengeti each group of male cheetahs may have a dry season territory and many kilometres away another territory which they inhabit during the rainy season. The same is probably true of females. Certainly one female cheetah which I knew appeared yearly in the same dry season territory, but I never discovered where she went during the rains. Most likely, as is true of other cheetahs, she moved to the open plains, to which almost all the gazelles had migrated at that time of year.

On one occasion I was puzzled to see three resident male cheetahs chasing a female off their territory. One would expect males to encourage a female to stay in their territory, but perhaps she was their sister and so this aggression was a way nature had developed to stop inbreeding. Perhaps they simply could not tolerate hunting competition within their territory.

I followed one particular cheetah many years ago, convinced it must be sick. It would repeatedly chase herds of Thomson gazelles, but never succeeded in catching anything, for it did not seem to be able to run at full speed. Furthermore, after each chase, it lay down to rest, as if tired. Finally though, after one such rest, it got up, walked fifty metres and picked up a gazelle fawn. I became suspicious. Was this coincidence or was it a hunting technique? Determined to find the answer I followed the cheetah over a number of days and discovered its system. It would frighten the herd, then lie down and wait. If the herd had a fawn, the youngster would lie absolutely motionless for half an hour or so, but then raise its head slightly to look around. This is what the cheetah was waiting for, and, of course, once it knew where the youngster was hiding it had an easy prey.

Cheetahs, unlike the other cats, do not have retractable claws and in this respect are more like dogs, although in cheetahs the dew claw is sharp and is apparently used to hold the prey. Their normal hunting technique depends on running speed. The cheetah is the fastest land mammal and can reach a speed of about a hundred kilometres per hour. However, unlike the dog family, it does not run over large distances but can only keep up its tremendous speed for a hundred metres or so. To get close enough to its intended prey, usually adult gazelles, it utilises the technique it inherited from its ancestors: stealth. Lions, leopards and cheetahs all creep up on their prey, but while the lion and leopard cannot run at full speed for more than thirty or forty metres and so have to get very close to their prey before running or very occasionally pouncing on it, the cheetah can start its run at a far greater distance. Once a cheetah catches up with its prey, it uses a forepaw to hit one of the prey's hind legs. The victim is thrown off balance, and the cheetah applies the throat bite. This is quite a feat when one considers the speed at which both predator and prey are running: a Thomson gazelle can reach seventy kilometres per hour. Cheetahs have evolved a sort of anti-skidding ridge on the pads of their paws. Lions do not have this refinement and I remember once seeing a lioness take off from rocky ground in order to pursue a zebra and promptly slip and tumble on to her side with a tremendous thump.

While the slenderly built cheetahs normally prey on small and medium-sized animals, they will occasionally tackle large animals such as zebras and wildebeests. The first apparent proof I got of this was in 1962 when I suddenly came across a group of four cheetahs eating a zebra. Unfortunately the cheetahs were shy and immediately ran off. This did, however, give me the opportunity of inspecting the zebra. The cheetahs had barely started their meal and I found the zebra's body was still warm and had bite marks on its throat. It was inconceivable that the cheetahs had taken the kill over from lions or even a

TOP: The long vegetation of a marsh near my camp provides an ideal spot for a lioness to hide her newborn cubs where they are less likely to be found by hyaenas or leopards.

BOTTOM: Able to run within minutes of being born, fleeing is the wildebeest's main means of avoiding becoming a victim to the pursuit of a predator.

Egrets catch insects
disturbed by a large creature
walking through the grass
and often, when the birds
have eaten enough, they
'hitch a ride' on their large
companion's back.

Impala and many other
mammals tolerate tickbirds
which remove insects and
warn their hosts of danger.

ABOVE: Dikdiks escape from predators by running away among thick vegetation and then lying motionless on the ground. This escape technique was probably used by the forest ancestors of all antelopes.

RIGHT: Dikdiks, pigmy antelopes about the size of hares, with small proboscis-like noses, use glands situated below the eyes to mark their territory.

powerful leopard and so I felt sure they had killed the zebra themselves. At the time no one believed me, but since then a number of people, including myself, have seen cheetahs kill large prey.

For some years an interesting female cheetah roamed the area near my camp at Lake Ndutu. When searching for prey she would climb a tree and survey the area. If she saw nothing then she would clamber down, walk for fifty metres or so and climb another tree. This is a pattern of behaviour used by leopards today and probably also by the cheetah's ancestors when they lived in the forest.

Normally cheetahs are open country animals, but this female seemed to live most of the time in the acacia tree country and had developed a hunting technique suited to her surroundings. The lake near my camp is surrounded by bush and woodland, an isolated patch in the middle of vast plains. This gives me ample opportunity to observe the species which have adapted to this habitat.

4. Bush and Woodland

The ungulate species found in bush and woodland areas can be the same or similar to some of those found in forests or in open plains country but many are specific to bush country. Where did they come from? Did their ancestors move straight from the forest into bush country or did some of them first live on the open plains before moving into bush country? In observing the behaviour of animal species which live in acacia tree and bush country, I have come to the conclusion that it is probably possible to determine the sequence of events with a fair degree of accuracy. If the animals living in bush country are solitary or live in pairs, like their forest ancestors, they probably moved straight from the forest into bush country; if they live in herds, like open country animals, they probably lived on the plains first. Because a herd can be spotted much more easily by predators than a lone animal or a pair and running away among bushes can hinder speed, any ungulate continuing to live in a herd in bush country must somehow cope with this problem.

Impala are an interesting example of herd-living animals which have developed an effective escape mechanism. When a predator tries to catch an impala, all the members of the herd make tremendous zigzagging leaps around each other. The height of the leaps is a protection in itself, but the zigzagging must make it very difficult for the predator to concentrate on any pre-selected individual.

I love watching impala. With their long slender legs and bodies they are the most graceful of antelopes and when the sun starts to set their chestnut coloured coats seem to glow in the darkening landscape.

Impala divide into distinct adult male and female herds, a lone male being in charge of the latter. He usually has a full time job keeping rival males at bay and ensuring that no females run off. As a result he normally becomes exhausted after some weeks or months and, losing out to a rival, he rejoins the male herd, has a long rest and may then try to regain possession of the female herd.

Among the male group individuals often fight, banging their gracefully curved horns together. These fights are usually in play. Play has a useful function for it gives individuals a chance to discover their relative strengths, making serious fights, during which they might be badly hurt, less frequent.

One of my favourite antelopes living in bush country is the dikdik, which is no larger than a hare. In behaviour dikdiks are very much like their forest ancestors and the present day duikers and, this, taken together with the fact that they normally live in pairs within a territory, have one offspring at a time and, like duikers, hide by lying down, leads me to the conclusion that their

OPPOSITE: A honey badger or ratel may attack large creatures – in this case my car. I don't know why but it was courting a female and may have felt I was too close.

177

ancestors moved straight from the forest into bush country. I have spent quite a bit of time watching and following these dainty antelopes, partly because it used to be believed that they only lived in pairs. However, near my camp I have a number of times come across as many as five together. Subsequently I discovered that males may sometimes have two females, each with an offspring. It was also said that only the males mark their territory, by stroking fluid from a gland situated under the eyes on to twigs, but I have also noted a female marking her territory. Another marking behaviour used by dikdik is explained in a different way by an African story.

'One day, a long time ago, a little dikdik was walking along his little path through the bushes. Abruptly, when he went around a corner, he tripped over an enormous elephant dropping. The dikdik was extremely angry that the elephant could be so bad mannered and inconsiderate as to defecate on his path. Ever since then the dikdik has been trying to take revenge: he always defecates in the same spot, hoping that one day the elephant will trip over the pile.'

Other pigmy antelopes, such as steinbucks, also live in bush country. They are similar in behaviour to dikdiks, except that steinbucks will occasionally move into open country, something I have never seen a dikdik do.

The creatures which prey on these antelopes include black-backed jackals, serval cats, caracals, which are the African version of the lynx, and leopards.

Many years ago I spent six months following a female leopard and her one-and-a-half-year-old cub. At the time leopards had hardly been studied at all and so it was exciting work because almost any activity I saw provided new information. Action was not frequent because leopards spend most of their time sleeping. All the same, when they do do something it is fascinating to watch.

Leopards are basically forest animals. At the same time they are very adaptable and have expanded into a wide variety of habitats. The snow leopard which lives high up in the Himalayas is an extreme example. In East Africa leopards occur in forests and in any landscape which has some cover. Their superb camouflage even allows them to live very close to towns. Anyone who has never actually seen a leopard in the wild before is unlikely to spot one even though it may only be a few metres away. The first one I saw was pointed out to me by a park ranger but for the first thirty seconds I saw nothing, although the leopard was lying on an almost bare branch only fifteen metres in front of me.

Many years later I had an argument with a scientist who had been studying chimpanzees in the forest every day for two years and who stated there were no leopards in that forest. I disagreed but he insisted that it was impossible that over a two year period he should not have seen a leopard nor heard it nor found its tracks. I still disagreed but I am sure that he thought I must be stupid. A week later a leopard walked through the camp!

The female leopard I was watching and her one-and-a-half-year-old male cub would sometimes play together but when resting they would usually lie apart. This was quite different from lions, who like to lie together.

Surprisingly I never saw the leopard cub hunt seriously, even though he was equal in size to his mother. He relied completely on his mother for food. When the mother went hunting the cub would remain behind, lying in a tree or among some thick vegetation on the ground.

The mother's normal hunting method was to walk for thirty or fifty metres, then climb a tree and look around: the same system as that used by the female cheetah which lived in the acacia tree country. However, while the cheetah would soon move on if she saw nothing, the leopard usually lay down on a branch and looked as if she had given up the thought of hunting. Nothing could be further from the truth. As she lay there she was carefully watching for any movement in the landscape. She usually remained in the tree for at least half an hour and sometimes as much as an hour. If by that time she had seen nothing, she moved on for fifty to a hundred metres, climbed another tree and repeated the process. One day as I was following her it became obvious she had seen something. She stared hard, silently descended her tree and crept stealthily through the grass. I presumed she was creeping up on a hare and sure enough a grey form suddenly dashed from cover. The leopard pursued it and I kept my camera aimed at them, ready for the moment when both would be close together and clearly visible. This was about to happen when I was thrown completely off course. The hare suddenly dashed up a steep tree! I stared in amazement. The leopard quickly followed it up the tree and caught it. Only then did I realise it was not a hare but a wild cat of similar colour and size.

Leopards are opportunists and will eat almost anything they can catch: snakes, birds, rodents, hares, jackals, monkeys, gazelles and occasionally creatures as large as a wildebeest or zebra. They will also kill and eat lion cubs.

The stealth of a leopard when creeping up on its prey has to be seen to be believed. I remember once following the female when she saw a male Thomson gazelle grazing in the shade of a lone tree about a hundred metres away. The green grass was less than two centimetres high over the total distance. I was surprised that she decided to attempt to creep up on the gazelle: I didn't think she had a chance of getting close. Yet she soon got to within thirty metres, only moving forward when the gazelle lowered its head and started to graze. The next twenty metres took half an hour or more, the leopard slowly creeping forward on her tummy. Frequently the gazelle looked up and the leopard would freeze and wait. When the leopard was within ten metres and almost ready to run forward, the gazelle looked around and stared straight at her. The leopard froze. The gazelle continued to stare. Then I noticed that very, very slowly, millimetre by millimetre, the leopard was flattening herself. I was amazed at how flat she could make herself. The gazelle continued to graze. Now the leopard was being cautious. She remained lying flat, watching the gazelle. The

I discovered that tickbirds often drink a giraffe's saliva. Usually a giraffe does not object but in this case the giraffe poked its tongue at the bird, trying to keep it at bay.

Giraffes fight by hitting at each other with their stumpy horns. Such fights are rarely serious, but one giraffe has been observed to knock out another for fifteen minutes.

gazelle looked up briefly, walked away a few metres, then continued to graze. The leopard again crept forward. But then the gazelle again looked up and the leopard froze. This time, instead of continuing to graze, the gazelle slowly wandered away. It was obvious that this had nothing to do with the leopard. Purely by coincidence the gazelle had chosen that moment to move to the shade of another lone tree about fifty metres away. It was still not out of danger, because the leopard followed. Once more the predator got very close. For this particular Thomson gazelle, however, it was a lucky day. Just as the leopard was within striking distance, another male Thomson gazelle started walking towards them. The leopard flattened itself. The new gazelle arrived and displaced the other from the shade of the tree. Now the leopard concentrated on the new gazelle and a few minutes later caught it.

Once she had killed any prey about the size of a gazelle, the first thing the mother leopard did was to take it up a suitable tree to hide it from vultures, which might in turn attract hyaenas. The tree might be as much as three hundred metres from where she had made the kill and this manoeuvre often involved a considerable effort. Once the kill was safely stored, the leopard would rest for a while, then descend the tree and return to where she had left her large cub. Calling the cub she would lead it back to the kill.

On one occasion I found the mother leopard with a large kill, a wildebeest. It was too big for her to drag up a tree, so she did something extraordinary. She removed the stomach contents, then dragged the carcass for thirty metres to a very small tree. Then she reached up and bent this tree, breaking it at the base, so that its vegetation covered the carcass from view. It was amazingly effective. Numerous vultures found the stomach contents but none saw the carcass.

Of course vultures can easily see carcasses in trees. But I have never seen a vulture attempt to scavenge from one. Maybe they have difficulty in seeing leopards and will not risk tangling with them. While vultures must realise that any carcass in a tree belongs to a leopard and so avoid it, they would not normally associate a carcass on the ground with a leopard.

When lions and cheetahs make a kill, they eat as much as possible in one go and then leave the rest to the various scavengers, such as vultures, hyaenas and jackals. Leopards, however, having safely stored their food, may feed from a single kill over many days.

One of the escape systems used by some prey is warning calls. I have often seen silver-back jackals following a leopard for hundreds of metres while continually uttering their shrill, bark-like calls. Silver-back jackals may do the same to lions and cheetahs but with an interesting difference: they seldom follow the latter two predators and if they do, it is only over a short distance. Why this difference in response? Is it because leopards often prey on jackals while lions do not, or is it because leopards are so well camouflaged that they might creep back unseen? It is, of course, always safer to be able to see your opponent. Whatever the reason, it was useful for me to know that when the jackals called at night in this way, there was a leopard close by.

Another creature which utters harsh warning cries is the Guinea fowl. To my surprise I once saw a whole row of these birds in single file following the mother leopard, all screaming loudly. It was obvious from the leopard's looks and twitching tail tip that she did not like the disturbance at all. But there was nothing she could do about it. Ultimately the birds let the leopard proceed on her own, but by then every creature within a two kilometre radius knew there was a leopard around.

Probably the most extraordinary creature adapted to acacia tree country is the giraffe. Its great height and long neck enable it to reach vegetation out of reach of most other browsers, as well as helping it look out for lions which occasionally prey on adult giraffes. I have never personally seen a successful kill but am told that a lion will either chase a giraffe and hit a hind leg so that the giraffe loses its balance and crashes to the ground, or it will jump from a tree or small precipice on to a giraffe's back with the same result. Once the giraffe is lying on the ground and pretty helpless, the lion rushes up to its neck where it applies a throat bite. Tackling giraffes is a dangerous business for they have an extremely powerful kick which can knock a lion out and break its jaws.

Of course, as with the other herbivores, it is the new born which are especially at risk. I have filmed a giraffe birth, apparently the first time this had ever been done. I was taking my son, who was ten years old at the time, to the Olduvai Gorge where we had arranged to meet Mary Leakey and go searching for fossils. We passed a group of giraffes and Hugo said,

'Funny – one of those giraffes had some legs sticking out of its bottom.'

I stopped the car and turned back; sure enough, the giraffe was giving birth. I grabbed a film camera and we followed the giraffe. At first she was a little nervous but she soon calmed down and when the calf emerged, we were only thirty metres away. The mother remained standing while the new born calf landed with a tremendous crash on the ground and lay motionless. I cursed, thinking I had disturbed the birth and the youngster had been born dead. I felt guilty. Then suddenly the calf raised its head. Apparently this was quite difficult for its neck swayed back and forth like a snake. Finally, though, it managed to get up and, like a new born gazelle, lost its balance and toppled on to its side. It then repeatedly tried to get up but time and again fell over. After a few minutes it found the strength and balance to remain upright and then it suckled. When it had finished it followed its mother and they both disappeared among the bushes.

Giraffes live in herds but whether their ancestors lived in more open country, I do not know. I doubt they lived on the open plains because I suspect they were always browsers, eating leaves. Maybe, though, they lived in fairly open areas where there were plenty of trees.

Watching giraffes curl their long tongues around thorn-covered twigs and pulling them into their mouths between leathery lips is an amazing sight. It was while I was watching two giraffes feeding that I made an interesting discovery. As they fed, ten tickbirds landed on their backs, clambered up and down their bodies and long necks and fed on parasites which had been feeding from the giraffes. One of the birds, instead of feeding, pulled a beakful of hair out of one of the giraffes and then flew off to line its nest. The giraffe took no notice. One of the giraffes stopped feeding and stood immobile, looking into space. As it did so, one of the birds flew up to its head and landed on its lower lip, hanging on upside down. The bird then poked its head into the giraffe's mouth. I had often seen this in the past and assumed it was getting at parasites on the giraffe's lips but I now discovered what was really happening. The birds were drinking the giraffe's saliva. Normally the giraffes ignore the tickbirds but on this occasion, the giraffe pushed the bird away with its long tongue. The bird must have been thirsty, because it fluttered around the side of the giraffe's mouth, only to be pushed away once more. Again the bird fluttered around to get at the giraffe's mouth from a different angle, but now the giraffe extended its long tongue and kept the bird at bay, the wiggling tip of its tongue occasionally even pushing the hovering bird backwards. Finally the bird gave up and the giraffe continued to feed from a flat-topped acacia tree.

Soon afterwards the two giraffes stopped feeding. They stood close together and one of them swung its head round in a wide arc, audibly hitting the other in the neck with its blunt, stumpy horns. The other retaliated, and the two giraffes continued to hit each other for some minutes. This behaviour, called necking, is quite common and seems to be play fighting: serious fights appear to be extremely rare among giraffes although on one occasion a giraffe knocked his opponent out for a quarter of an hour.

Giraffes are not the only large creatures which live in bush country. Buffalo and rhino also inhabit these areas, but these two species seem equally at home in the forest and to some extent in open country. I recently saw a rhino with a calf charge a buffalo. The buffalo, taken completely unawares, only ran away when the rhino was almost on top of it. However, the rhino soon stopped and then, to my surprise, the buffalo also stopped and continued to graze as if nothing had happened. The mother rhino, followed by her calf, charged again. This time the buffalo lowered its horns at the oncoming rhinos and calmly stood its ground. I expected a gory fight. When the rhino's horn was about to hit the buffalo, however, the rhino wheeled to the side and trotted off. The buffalo once again calmly continued to graze.

One might expect rhinos to have no enemies, apart from man, but spotted hyaenas may attack a calf. Although the mother rhino will try to defend her calf by attacking a spotted hyaena, she is just not fast enough to catch it.

While spotted hyaenas occur in both open country and bush country, the striped hyaena occurs almost exclusively in bush country. They are rarely seen, not because they are uncommon but because their stripes are superb camouflage, the more so since a striped hyaena will stand absolutely immobile when it senses danger. Should danger approach too close then the striped hyaena will erect its splendid mane, which makes it look much larger than it really is and so help to frighten off an opponent.

Large parts of Africa are not covered by open plains, forest, or bush and acacia tree country but by miombo woodland. In this type of habitat most if not all of the trees are fire-resistant hardwoods which are thornless, well spaced and often no more than thirty metres high. Miombo woodland may have evolved no more than 12,000 years ago as a result of man starting to burn large areas on a yearly or almost yearly basis.

Because miombo woodland contains fairly unpalatable grasses and most leaves grow out of reach of most herbivores, and because it is a new habitat, it does not contain as great a variety of species as most other types of African country. Fewer animal species have had time to adjust to it. Those that have include elephant, rhino, buffalo, impala and also roan and sable antelopes. In addition most of the carnivores inhabit miombo woodland.

Some years ago I joined a group to penetrate deep into the miombo woodlands of the Selous Game Reserve, the largest uninhabited wild area in Tanzania. Among the group were Brian Nicholson, who had been the game warden for this area for over thirty years; Peter Matthiessen, the renowned author; and Tom Arnold, who is a Member of Parliament in England but has a great love for Africa and who instigated the expedition. Although tourists visit a small part of this reserve north of the Rufiji River, the very much larger southern part can only be explored by organising a full scale expedition. We were able to use four wheel drive vehicles for the first two days by following a dirt track which leads south to the heart of the Selous but the track ends where the Mbarangandu and Luwegu Rivers meet. Any further progress is only possible on foot.

Travelling on foot through wild country is a wonderful experience: one sees many more insects and other interesting small creatures. To minimise the amount of equipment the porters – and the rest of us – had to carry, we did not take tents but slept in the open under the stars. As we fell asleep we could clearly hear the chirping of crickets intermingled with frogs croaking and hippos bellowing in the river. Every now and then we also heard the roaring of a lion and remembered that man-eaters used to be common in this area and maybe still are. Probably they had been wounded at some stage by hunters. Anyway, during the night, someone regularly woke up and added wood to the fire and Brian Nicholson kept a gun by his side. It was the first time that I had had a gun as protection in the wild. Although it was quite reassuring, at the same time I felt it distanced us from nature. We seemed to be intruders rather than a part of it.

My main aim during that expedition was to photograph the elusive greater

OVERLEAF: (p. 186): A leaf-nosed bat, like other bats, uses a radar system to identify objects, including prey. A more primitive and less efficient echo location system may be used by some species of shrew.

OVERLEAF (p. 187): A patas monkey surveys its open country surroundings. This species spends much time on the ground and has evolved long legs to enable it to run faster from predators and reach the safety of trees.

Serious fights between
hippos are common and
cause more deaths than
lions, which occasionally
prey on the large creatures
when they come on to land
at night to feed.

kudu and sable antelopes, which I had only rarely seen before, and also the Nyasa wildebeest which has an attractive white stripe over its nose and which I had never encountered before.

I also spent a great deal of time watching and photographing the hippos which occurred in great numbers in the rivers and surrounding pools. Where there are many hippos territorial fights may occur and I saw a number of these. In addition there often seemed to be tension among a normally friendly group which resulted in squabbles. I then noticed something interesting. Almost invariably during a squabble the subordinate animal would turn its rump toward the dominant one and defecate. As it did so it would frantically wag its tail and so splash its dung into the dominant one's face. Hardly a friendly action, one would think! However, I came to the conclusion that the subordinate was trying, through its recognisable smell, to show it was a member of the same group while at the same time indicating that it accepted its antagonist as dominant.

Hippos' main potential predators are crocodiles and lions, but they are protected from the former by their size and from the latter by living in water for most of the time. However, at night, when it is cool, they emerge to feed on land and are sometimes killed by lions. I have found lions eating a hippo but have never seen them kill one and wonder how they manage to tackle such a large creature. Crocodiles sometimes take young hippos but I have never seen them tackle a fully grown one.

I remember once seeing a hippo entering a river on the Serengeti. As a crocodile swam slowly past, the hippo paused and turned so that it remained facing the crocodile. The crocodile was about twice the length of the hippo and, as I was some distance away, I presumed the hippo was a youngster. When I looked more closely I found that the hippo was fully grown. This meant that the crocodile was six metres or so in length, almost two metres longer than any other I had seen.

There are not many rivers on the Serengeti but they contain some of the largest crocodiles in Africa, probably because there is so much prey and the crocodiles have plenty to eat.

During the dry season most of the rivers dry up, but small stretches retain water and, as might be expected, contain numerous crocodiles. I once walked for some kilometres along a dry stretch of a river bed. Every now and then I came across small muddy pools only a couple of square metres in area. Undoubtedly these attracted animals which wanted to drink. Many, however, contained a large lone crocodile whose length almost filled the pool.

I spent many days waiting at one stretch of river which contained some water and numerous large crocodiles. Animals regularly came to drink there. From the behaviour of the drinking animals it seemed that the individuals resident in the area were cautious when approaching the water and those that were not resident were far less cautious. This made sense because crocodiles

OPPOSITE: A white-fronted bee-eater, having caught a butterfly, returns to one of the perches from which it waits for insects to fly past.

191

do not occur on most of the Serengeti and so many of the migrating animals are hardly or not at all aware of danger in the water.

I have read stories of crocodiles using their tails to hit a drinking animal into the water but have never seen this myself nor do I know if it is true. It might be, for I have had a young monitor lizard repeatedly whip my hand with its long tail. In all cases I saw, the crocodiles slowly swam towards a drinking animal, often with only their eyes and the tip of their nose just visible. During the many days I stayed at the river watching crocodiles I never saw a kill. Where the gazelles drank, the water was so shallow that the crocodiles could not get close enough without becoming fully visible. Instead they waited, apparently hoping one of the gazelles would enter the water a bit as they often do when drinking. Then one day a waterbuck came down to drink. To my surprise none of the crocodiles moved towards it, even though they had approached every other creature. More surprisingly still, the waterbuck calmly and slowly crossed the river and no crocodile took any notice. I wondered why. A hunter once told me that when he shot a waterbuck for food he had to be very careful when cleaning it. Apparently the waterbuck has some glands which are extremely distasteful. I came to the conclusion therefore that these glands must have evolved in order to repel crocodiles. This enables waterbuck when pursued by man or dogs, to escape by jumping into the water and swimming away. This is not true of other antelopes and gazelles. When danger threatens almost all species run away from water. This makes sense because usually near water the vegetation is thick, providing lots of cover for lions and leopards.

The vegetation and trees along rivers and gullies provide a habitat for forest species. Along a small stretch of one river on the Serengeti there are a number of troops of black and white colobus monkeys, a species normally associated with high altitude forests, the closest of which is at least a hundred and fifty kilometres away. Some monkey species have adapted completely to living away from thick forest. Vervets remain very close to trees but patas monkeys and baboons often wander quite far into the open. Patas monkeys have long legs which enable them to run fast and baboons are protected by the large and powerful males in charge of the troop. The olive baboons, which occur on the Serengeti and elsewhere, eat fruit, seeds, leaves and insects but they also regularly prey on gazelle fawns and other small mammals.

It used to be believed that man was the only primate which regularly ate meat, having started the habit when he moved on to the open plains and started to scavenge as a prelude to hunting. This supposition appears to be wrong. I feel sure man was a hunter before he moved on to the open plains and, furthermore, was a hunter before he also became a scavenger. To get clues on the behaviour of prehistoric man we must look at the behaviour of the apes and of man today. Where both show the same behaviour, it is likely that this was shared by their ancestors.

5. Apes and Man

Filming the behaviour of chimpanzees has, to some extent, been my life's work. Over the past twenty-three years, I have spent six years in the forest among the chimpanzees and taken a total of one hundred hours of film. Since then I have spent three and a half years editing the material into a two hour feature film.

I started filming the wild chimpanzees in 1962 on behalf of the National Geographic Society who wanted a record of Jane Goodall's study of these creatures. She had been studying the chimpanzees for eighteen months by the time I arrived and although over that period the chimpanzees had slowly started to trust her, they certainly did not accept anyone else. As a result the first three months were exceedingly frustrating because the chimpanzees immediately fled when they saw me, even if I was as much as a kilometre away. I tried using hides but the chimpanzees' eyesight was so good that they invariably spotted me. Their shyness also created another problem. In order to get them used to me I had to work alone, carrying all my equipment myself in the mountainous country. This included a film camera, a heavy wooden tripod, a bulky 600mm lens and a rucksack filled with other lenses and spare film. I also carried a tin of food and a small amount of water. Drinking was no great problem because of the various small streams. I was lucky in that three of the male chimpanzees were much less shy and in fact they occasionally visited the camp where they were given bananas in order to hasten their habituation to humans. The other chimpanzees eventually followed these three males' example and so very slowly over the next years the chimpanzees came to accept both Jane and me, ultimately to such a degree that it was possible to follow them in the forest and finally even get within touching distance. The longest period I spent in one stretch in the forest was a year. The other periods varied from three to nine months. As a result I got to know the individual chimpanzees better than I know any humans and could recognise each individual from a kilometre away and more. This may sound incredible but each individual is physically different and many also move in slightly different ways. Of course few humans could recognise their friends from that distance. But if one lived in the wild and it was important to recognise friends from a great distance, one would find it was not too difficult.

Apart from being physically different each chimpanzee has his or her own distinct personality and in filming I soon concentrated most of my efforts on one interesting family. It consisted of the old mother, named Flo, who was about forty years old, her two sons, twelve-year-old Faben and eight-year-old

OPPOSITE: An old female chimpanzee, named Flo, catches termites which, in defence of their nest, bite on to the pieces of grass poked into a small hole in a termite mound by the chimpanzee. Chimpanzees are not only tool users but also tool makers, since they will change the shape of natural objects in order to make them suitable for a specific purpose. For instance they will also use a twig for termiting but make it suitable first by stripping it of leaves and breaking it to an appropriate length.

While chimpanzees may rest on the ground during daytime, at night they sleep in nests, making a new one every evening. It only takes minutes for a chimpanzee to construct a nest by bending over leafy branches or palm fronds.

199

Figan, and her daughter Fifi, five years old. She soon gave birth to another son, named Flint. The relationships within the family were fascinating. Flo's juvenile daughter, Fifi, was absolutely fascinated by the new baby and continually wanted to look at him, touch him and if possible hold him. Flo's sub-adult son, Faben, was a calm and easy going individual, old enough to leave the family for long periods in order to search for food or to accompany one or more adult males as they visited distant parts of the community's territory. Flo's adolescent son, Figan, was too young to leave the family except occasionally for a short period, yet he continually behaved as if he was tough. As in human teenagers he was obviously going through a difficult and frustrating period: for instance, if he acted big, displaying his strength near the adults, they were liable to beat him up and so he had to contain himself.

I decided that the relationships between the members of this chimpanzee family would make an unusual film, especially if I could cover the developments over a decade or so. As it turned out the film would cover over twenty years and as the time approached to start editing, I returned to the forest to get some up to date film material. The old mother Flo had died. Fifi was twenty-seven years old and had three children while her brother Figan had become the dominant male of their community of about fifty members.

The physical development of chimpanzees is very similar to that of humans. Thus a female can have her first child at about thirteen or fourteen years old. Yet neither females nor males look fully adult until they are about eighteen to twenty years old. Furthermore the female's sexual cycle lasts roughly a month and pregnancy just under nine months. The gap between the birth of children can be three years for a young female and increases to five years as a female becomes older. This would seem to be different from humans but in fact is similar to the time when human mothers, like chimpanzees, used to continue suckling their children for a number of years. Since continued suckling can act as a contraceptive this results in births being spread out.

The morning after I arrived I got up before dawn and set off into the forest, looking forward to meeting my chimpanzee friends again. I was lucky, for I soon came across Fifi and her family. Her son Freud was now an adolescent. He was sitting staring fixedly and in apparent admiration at a large and powerful male. Typical adolescent behaviour. The male ignored Freud, which was also typical. Further away in the forest Fifi's juvenile son Frodo was throwing stones at a 1.5 metre long monitor lizard. Frodo is a little devil and throws stones at almost everyone. He then went over to his small sister Fanny, picked her up by one leg, held her upside down and bounced her head on the ground. Fanny never seems to be quite sure whether her brother Frodo is being aggressive or just playing rough, though she seems to accept that it is merely play. Nearby Fifi ignored her children. She acts as if she believes that her children must learn early to cope with life. She may have learnt this from her mother, Flo, who used to be the same. As Fifi gets older she spends more and more time staring into space as if daydreaming. I wish I could look into her mind. Can she remember far into the past when she was young and when her mother was alive?

Fifi's apparent daydreaming was disturbed when suddenly we heard other chimpanzees calling in the distance. She and her family replied, pouting their lips and hooting. I knew that the distant chimpanzees were other members of Fifi's fifty-strong community. I would probably see some of them later.

A chimpanzee community can be compared to a small human community. Each individual knows all the others but each may wander around alone or together with one or more family members or friends as they visit widely spread fruiting trees and so on. Within a family the relationship between a mother and her children is very strong and lasts throughout life. Thus although adult sons or daughters may wander around alone or with non family members, they regularly rejoin their mother – they visit her, in effect. Adult daughters may in fact spend most of their time with their mother, but adult sons spend most of their time with the big males or with sexually attractive females.

The relationship between brothers and sisters also lasts for life. Adult brothers, for instance, will support each other during squabbles with other members of the community. However, as with humans, the relationships within each family differ: in some they are close, in others more distant.

Although adult males interact regularly with the female members of the community, they tend to prefer the company of other males. Not so different from humans, when one considers men visiting pubs or going to their clubs to meet friends.

Adult female chimpanzees tend to be slightly more solitary than males although this of course changes when a female has children. This also appears to have a human parallel. In general more women than men seem to be able to cope with being alone.

Because female chimpanzees tend to wander around alone their first child may lead a fairly lonely life until the next child is born. Subsequently her children tend to play together and this probably lays the basis for the strong bonds between brothers and sisters. Sometimes a number of adult females may meet and as a result all their children can have a wonderful time playing together although, as with human children, little squabbles occur. Nevertheless, when a mother wants to leave, her child may well want to continue playing and a mother may have to grab her child and literally drag it away.

It is rare to see a mother physically punish a badly behaved child. Usually she will tickle the child and distract its attention from what it is doing. When a mother does hit her child she always immediately reassures it afterwards, usually by hugging it.

If this system was always used by human mothers, a lot more children would grow up with more self-confidence. As a result they would have a chance of becoming less troubled adults. This does not mean that all adult chimpanzees are confident, but their lack of confidence is usually a result of other traumatic events, especially the death of their mother when they are young. Such orphans often develop nervous ticks which last all their life. I know one individual who continually pushes his lips in and out, in effect making sucking movements, and his older sister repeatedly makes a sucking sound.

Within a chimpanzee community there is a dominance hierarchy among both males and females. As in humans, some individuals have a strong urge to dominate while others are easy going. Some are aggressive, others more timid or nervous. Of course the hierarchy in a community may change. The dominant individual may be deposed by a subordinate or there may be changes lower down in the hierarchy. To reach a higher status in the hierarchy, individuals may form alliances and support each other. A subordinate may become number two by becoming friends with the top individual. The same is of course true in humans. Changes in the hierarchy can cause a problem for individuals who have been away for any length of time, because they will not know who has become dominant during their absence. In humans this can be found out by word of mouth. Chimpanzees do not have this capability: they must find out by body language. I witnessed such an event that day in the forest.

By this time more chimpanzees, both males and females with youngsters, had joined Fifi and her family. All these individuals had apparently seen each other recently for their meetings were peaceful, consisting of greetings such as embracing, kissing and in one case a male kissing a female's hand. Suddenly, however, I heard excited hooting and saw a large group of males coming down the slope of a mountain. The chimpanzees I was with immediately responded by hooting themselves. It seemed as if everyone was very excited at seeing one another again, and probably they were. Some females started to approach the arriving males in order to greet them. However they soon clambered up trees when they saw the males starting to charge with all their hair erect. This made them look twice their normal size.

There was pandemonium as the males charged around showing off their immense strength by stamping on the ground, throwing large rocks and grabbing small trees or branches which they swung back and forth forcefully. They also charged each other, trying to impress and frighten their opponents. I noticed that two males had joined each other to confront another one. I knew the two were brothers, and one of them had been among the new arrivals. The screams and hoots were ear-piercing and added to the confusion, helping to scare the more nervous individuals.

On this occasion there were no fights. This is often the case. It is all a big show and it is often the individual who makes the most noise who becomes dominant. It reminds one of human politics, with the show of strength, the bluff and of course the biggest, loudest mouth being major elements in becoming dominant. Forming alliances is also important. Unlike brothers, who invariably support each other, the alliances formed between others are not necessarily

dependable because friends can be fickle and switch their support to the winning side. The frustration shown by a male losing a friend on whose support he thought he could count needs to be seen to be believed.

Once the displays have sorted out the dominance hierarchy, the subordinate males must normally show acceptance of their relative status by making submissive gestures to the dominant male. Bowing is a common example. In response the dominant male may reassure his subordinate by touching or patting him. Or he may haughtily ignore him.

The submissive gestures made to the dominant male normally calm him down quickly. To calm him down even more the other males may start to groom him. Grooming is the equivalent of stroking and as such primarily a calming gesture which relaxes the recipient. Stroking in humans undoubtedly evolved from grooming. Chimpanzees also use grooming to clean each other, but contrary to popular belief wild chimpanzees do not have fleas. They are removing tiny bits of vegetation, grains of sand or skin flakes.

The greeting gestures of chimpanzees are the same as those found in humans and give clues as to where our greeting gestures came from. Greetings are basically derived from submissive gestures and from reassurance gestures. Physical touch is reassuring. We automatically touch or embrace someone who is frightened. In chimpanzee greetings, embracing is mutually reassuring and is derived from the mother-infant bond. Kissing is also mutually reassuring and is derived from a small infant taking its first solid food from the mother's mouth. Hand-kissing, hand-holding and patting are due to a subordinate being too scared to approach closely and asking to be reassured by holding out his hand; the dominant chimpanzee responds by a reassuring kiss, touch or pat. Hand-shaking is similar to the previous situation except that one holds on to the other's hand while it is being patted. Bowing is derived from the submissive gesture seen in many animals, namely crouching low in front of a dominant individual. There is one greeting in chimpanzees which at first I could not relate to humans. It is when one reassures another by holding his scrotum. I then discovered that this greeting used to exist among humans not so long ago and is described in ancient manuscripts. In the Bible it was tactfully translated, being described as putting the hand on the thigh.

As I sat in the forest, I heard some chimpanzees laughing and turned around to see some infants tickling each other as they played next to the adult female, Little Bee. She watched them and then joined in, tickling one of the youngsters in its groin. He roared with laughter and struggled as if trying to get away. But when Little Bee stopped tickling him, he grabbed her hand and pulled it to his neck, asking her to tickle him there. Little Bee responded. She is a wonderful mother who seems to love all youngsters. She had a rough youth herself for she was born with a club foot and often had great difficulty in keeping up with her mother. Little Bee's mother had come from the neighbouring community and was treated as a bit of an outsider, especially by the other females who

OPPOSITE: Infant chimpanzees, when very young, cling on to their mother's tummy. Later they ride on her back, sometimes until they are four or five years old. During alarming situations, however, they will still transfer to their mother's tummy where they are more protected and less of an obstruction if their mother wants to flee through undergrowth.

often chased her away or even attacked her. This did not make Little Bee's life any easier as a youngster, but as she grew up she became completely integrated into this community.

As in small primitive human communities such as those in New Guinea or in the Amazon, neighbouring communities of chimpanzees are aggressive towards one another. Thus any male chimpanzee entering the neighbouring community's territory risks a serious and possibly fatal attack. While females may become members of a neighbouring community, it is not clear how this happens because on some occasions neighbouring females are also attacked.

Most attacks involve tearing out hair, stamping on each other and biting. Adult male chimpanzees are about four times as strong as a man, which gives some idea of the force that can be employed in attacks. In addition chimpanzees will use weapons: they often throw large stones or rocks and will use sticks as clubs. This makes them tool users. More importantly they are also tool makers. The difference between the two is that a tool user may merely use an object at hand in its unchanged form while a tool maker changes the object first. Chimpanzees, finding water in a hole in a tree and unable to reach it with their lips, will crumple some leaves in their mouth and use them as an efficient sponge. They will also fashion a tool by stripping leaves off a twig or breaking a piece of grass to the required length and poking the made tool into one of the small holes in a termite mound. The termites in defence of their nest bite on to the twig or grass and so the chimpanzees can extract them and eat them.

It used to be believed that chimpanzees were purely vegetarians, but in fact they regularly hunt young bushbuck, bushpigs, baboons and monkeys. A number of chimpanzees may co-operate during a hunt: one or two individuals will approach the quarry while others cut off the means of escape. When chimpanzees have meat they can be very aggressive and the closest I have come to being attacked seriously by a wild chimpanzee was while it was eating meat. Apparently meat is a prized possession and if a chimpanzee, even a subordinate one, feels someone might take it away, he is likely to go into a rage. As a result even the dominant male in the community will not normally risk stealing meat. Instead he may ask for a share by holding out his hand, palm upwards. It is the same as the human begging gesture. In response the subordinate may tear off a piece of meat and hand it to the dominant male or may refuse to share.

Chimpanzees have a fascinating relationship with their prey. While I was watching Fifi and her family in the forest, a troop of baboons arrived. Fifi's son, Frodo, five years old, immediately went towards the baboons and started throwing stones at them. Surprisingly this didn't seem to worry the baboons too much. They are remarkably quick in their reactions and so had no difficulty in avoiding the stones. Then Frodo went up to one of the baboons, an individual equal to him in size, and started bashing him on the head with his fist. The baboon jumped at Frodo and soon the two were wrestling. It looked serious

OPPOSITE TOP: Some adult females are more tolerant of youngsters playing around them than others and this one, Madame Bee, who has a club foot, often likes to join in with their games. Like humans, each chimpanzee has its own distinct personality.

OPPOSITE BOTTOM: A female chimpanzee will give birth for the first time at about thirteen years old and produce a new infant once every three to five years until she dies which may be at the age of 40 or more. Here an adult daughter with an infant sits with her mother, about 33 years old, who also has an infant.

but in fact it was a game and soon Frodo was roaring with laughter as the baboon tickled him. If chimpanzees hunted baboons whenever they saw them this sort of interaction would not happen. All the same it is extraordinary to see predator and prey playing with each other.

Occasionally chimpanzees eat each other. The same is or used to be true of some human tribes. In chimpanzees cannibalism usually occurs when the members of one community catch a neighbouring female with an infant in which case they may eat the infant. However, one dominant female in Fifi's community became a habitual cannibal. Assisted by her large daughter she regularly grabbed small infants from the subordinate females within her community and ate them. The reason for this is not known. She had a somewhat mad look in her eyes but madness may not have been the reason: perhaps there was a threat of over-population in their territory and so by killing other infants she was increasing the chances of survival of her own. Ultimately both she and her daughter died of a strange wasting disease and their children became orphans. There was a touching end to this story. The daughter's female offspring adopted her grandmother's young son. In other words the niece adopted her uncle.

Given that chimpanzees are occasionally cannibalistic, it is not surprising that they will also eat human babies. Near the Gombe National Park lives an adult man who was attacked by chimpanzees when he was seven years old. Apparently the chimpanzees first grabbed his baby brother but when he defended the baby, the chimpanzees dropped the young infant and grabbed him instead. They then, and I quote his words, 'started to eat me'. By this time his parents had been alerted by his screams. They managed to save him, but part of his face had already been torn away. This event and the cannibalism are horrifying stories. However man's treatment of chimpanzees is as bad and much worse. In Central and West Africa mothers are eaten and infants are tied up and sold in the markets. I saw one such youngster. His fingers had been tied to his wrists with wire and left like that for three weeks. We kept track of him for ten years after we released him and he was still unable to straighten his wrists; probably he was never able to again.

I had now spent six out of twenty-three years filming the one community of wild chimpanzees but this did not mean that the film was ready. It now needed to be edited and so, although I wanted to stay in the forest or on the open plains of the Serengeti, I had to leave the wild for the first time in twenty-five years and work in a large city for an extended period. Little did I realise then that the editing and related post-production work would take over three years. However, the resulting film is undoubtedly my life's most important work: it not only covers over two decades among the chimpanzees and includes numerous amusing and also traumatic events, but also, by concentrating on one family, it gives one the feeling of watching the relationships, squabbles and traumas in a human family and I think conveys the

208

OPPOSITE: Chimpanzees often hunt creatures such as bushbuck fawns, young bushpigs, colobus monkeys and baboons. They will not normally scavenge, having only once been seen to steal a kill which they saw baboons make. This makes me believe that in evolution man was a hunter before he also became a scavenger.

impression that chimpanzees are basically a people of the forest.

Scientists who study animal behaviour are terrified of being anthropomorphic, giving human characteristics to other creatures. Without doubt I will be accused of this in some of my writing, so I must make clear that I admit that humans have a greater brain power than any other creatures on earth and as a result are different. However these differences did not appear out of mid-air but evolved from something that was already there. If one accepts this then the basic things, from which our differences evolved, are still likely to exist in some other creatures.

Because we share many basic behaviour patterns with the chimpanzees, and also with some other creatures, studies on their behaviour give us invaluable information on how our own prehistoric ancestors probably behaved. This supplements the discoveries of the fossil remains of prehistoric man which show to some extent what man's ancestors looked like but rarely give information on behaviour, certainly not emotional behaviour.

Man's ancestors started life in the forests and I imagine that, when they were still residing in the forests, they may already have had a social organisation like that of chimpanzees, namely a territorial community in which individuals could wander away from the group and search for food alone or with one or more other members of the community. Their main food was probably fruits, leaves, nuts, seeds and so on, but they probably already hunted small creatures. At night they probably behaved like chimpanzees, sleeping where they were when night fell and maybe also making sleeping platforms in the safety of trees. When they started leaving the forest to live on the open plains where they were more vulnerable to attack from predators, members of the community, and especially members of the same family, probably stayed together much more. In addition, instead of sleeping wherever they happened to be, all members of the community probably returned to a specific spot where there was greater safety. The smaller females would have needed the protection of the large males and to ensure that the males would not leave them for long, they became sexually attractive for most of the time, rather than for a few days per month. The ancestors of man would have had the ability to walk upright while they still lived in forests, but this became the norm on the plains, making it easier to spot danger, especially over high grass, and leaving the hands free to take food to a safe place and ultimately to carry stone weapons and tools. It is probable that, like chimpanzees, the ancestors of man made simple tools from vegetation before leaving the forests. They probably also stripped branches to use as clubs. Since many acacia trees and bushes have long sharp thorns, I suspect that the early hominids soon discovered that it was advantageous to leave the sharp thorns on their clubs. They would also have used stones for throwing in self-defence and ultimately as an aid in catching their prey. At first they would have used these stones as they found them on the ground, but later chipped and fashioned them into tools. I have found literally thousands

of stone tools on the Serengeti including bolas stones, hand axes and scrapers. The oldest, recognisable as tools, were made about two million years ago.

Within a prehistoric human group there would have been a dominance hierarchy in which subordinates would have had to acknowledge their superiors' dominance. Judging from the chimpanzees' behaviour this would have included bowing. I remember as a teenager at school being taught that hand-shaking evolved from showing that you had no weapon in your hand. Watching chimpanzee behaviour has shown that hand-shaking in fact evolved from one individual holding out a hand while begging for reassurance and another responding by holding and patting the hand. Other submissive and reassuring gestures one sees in chimpanzees indicate that prehistoric people almost certainly embraced, kissed and even kissed an outstretched hand.

My knowledge of the chimpanzee gestures gave a probable explanation for one of the most exciting prehistoric discoveries ever made: the three million year old hominid footprints, which were found by Mary Leakey and her team at Laetoli. It was in fact due to my son's interest in fossils that Mary Leakey's excavations at Laetoli took place. He had found some fossils in the gravel around Ndutu Lodge, not far from my camp. We asked the owner at the time, George Dove, where he collected his gravel and he referred us to a dry river bed some six kilometres away. Hugo and I went there and collected numerous fossils. We took these to show Mary Leakey, whose camp is some fifty kilometres from Lake Ndutu. She wondered where the river led, or in other words where the fossils were coming from. I suggested that I would take her to explore the place when my son returned from a visit to his mother in Dar es Salaam. However my son was delayed for two days and much to his disappointment we found on arrival at Ndutu that Mary had not waited for us but had explored the river bed with George Dove. It had led to Laetoli, which turned out to be an exceedingly rich fossil site, pre-dating the Olduvai Gorge by at least a million years, so that the fossils collected there belonged to creatures which lived about three and a half million years ago. In fact on that first trip Mary Leakey picked up two fossil hominid teeth.

A year later Mary Leakey started her excavations at Laetoli and I occasionally visited her and her team of scientists. One day I arrived and was shown a trail of footprints made by hominids over three million years ago. It was an amazing discovery. The prints looked exactly like those of present day humans. Most unexpected. It was exceedingly lucky that the prints had fossilised. It had happened because a nearby volcano was erupting dust at the time and subsequently a small shower of rain had fallen. Even the raindrops had left their marks in the muddy dust and been recorded for posterity. The footprints had been made by three individuals. The scientists told me that there was something strange about these prints which they could not figure out. Two individuals were walking side by side and the third was walking behind the larger of the two. What was strange was that the distances between the individuals did not vary at all as they walked along. The two walking parallel could be explained. If they were holding each other's hands they would remain at the same distance. But for the one behind to stay at the same distance he must have been holding on to the one in front of him. Why? The scientists thought he might have been blind and to test this theory they blindfolded one of their companions and had him hold on to another's shoulder while following him. Having heard this story I said,

'Actually he didn't have to be blind to act like that.' The scientists looked surprised and I explained, 'A scared chimpanzee will find reassurance, like man, by touching or holding on to a companion. When chimpanzees are walking away from danger one may walk behind the other and hold on to him. In this case these prehistoric humans were walking away from an erupting volcano which undoubtedly made them uneasy if not downright scared. So if I compared them to chimpanzees, I would expect them to be holding on to or at least touching each other.'

The scientists were excited, one of them calling it 'a brilliant deduction'. Actually if he had had a chance to watch chimpanzees as I have, he would have come to the same conclusion.

Mary Leakey has never publicised my son's role in the finding of the Laetoli fossil site. In her book *Disclosing the Past* she mentions another photographer as saying that the footsteps are comparable to the habit of young chimpanzees holding on to each other while playing 'follow my leader'. This explanation makes no sense.

It used to be believed that prehistoric man started eating meat as a scavenger. This is not true of chimpanzees, and is probably not true of man either. Chimpanzees are accomplished hunters and more importantly in this context will not eat a dead animal they find. Only on one occasion has a chimpanzee been seen to eat an animal not killed by himself or his companions, but it had seen a baboon make the kill and quickly appropriated it. Prehistoric people, like chimpanzees, would have co-operated with each other in hunting but, aided by their greater brain power and hunting tools, they would have developed more effective hunting strategies. The reason why most scientists believe that prehistoric man was a scavenger is that so much of his prey, as determined from fossil evidence, consisted of large animals. In fact, as when jackals and hyaenas attack large prey, these creatures often cannot react or move as fast as a smaller predator and can sometimes be easier to capture.

There is another clue to support my belief that prehistoric man may have hunted large animals. The extinction of many of the large prehistoric animals corresponds closely with the first appearance of stone tools, about two million years ago. Undoubtedly man also became a scavenger but I think he was mainly a hunter.

Of course as man invented new weapons which became accurate at greater and greater distances, he became the greatest predator of all time and the extinction of other species was accelerated. Early man's destruction of other species included some very much like him, such as *Zinjanthropus*, nicknamed the Nutcracker man, and also Neanderthal man. The only reason that the apes managed to avoid being exterminated by early man was that they lived in forests where they could escape among the thick vegetation and up trees. If they did not exist today, we would not know as much as we do about man himself.

One can have some idea of how much like man chimpanzees are if one considers that some captive chimpanzees have been taught three hundred words in sign language and can use these signs to converse rationally with their human companions. In fact, judging by their chemical make-up, genes, amino acids and many other factors, they are closer to man than they are to gorillas. What qualities must a living being have to be considered a human? If Neanderthal man or *Homo Habilis* lived today would he qualify? Or would the more brainy men of today have changed the rules to exclude them? I rather suspect so.

When Jane Goodall discovered that chimpanzees make tools, this caused some confusion in the scientific world. This was because the definition of man at that stage was 'the tool maker'. Of course the definition was quickly changed. One cannot imagine many humans and certainly not the church accepting chimpanzees as people. Yet I am sure that the chimpanzees even show the elementary beginnings of a religion. During thunder and lightning they often react with a powerful rhythmic display. It reminds one of a primitive tribe worshipping the god of thunder.

Most scientists and other people consider chimpanzees just another animal and as such feel they have the moral right to subject them to solitary confinement in zoos and laboratories and use them in painful medical experiments and chemical warfare. The chimpanzees that survive these traumas usually become mentally deranged. They are also used extensively as clowns and funny photographic subjects. In Europe, Spain has a particularly bad reputation in this respect. Some professional photographers there carry around a young chimpanzee and offer to take pictures of tourists with it. At the end of the summer season they drown the chimpanzee: buying a new one at the beginning of the next season is cheaper than feeding a chimpanzee through the winter months. Furthermore, as a chimpanzee reaches adolescence, it becomes physically powerful and therefore dangerous, especially because in frustration it is likely to erupt in fits of rage. Of course if a human is badly hurt as a result, the chimpanzee is likely to be killed. Modern knowledge of the resemblance of chimpanzees and other apes to man should surely guarantee them human-like rights: to be protected from torture, abuse and extermination.

While man's extermination of the animal species started with weapons, today it is more a result of his other inventions: axes, chemicals and machines tear down whole forests, exterminating not only the animal species living there

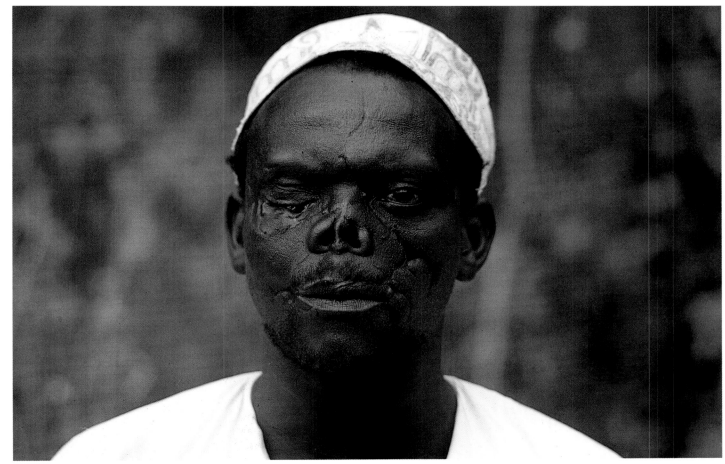

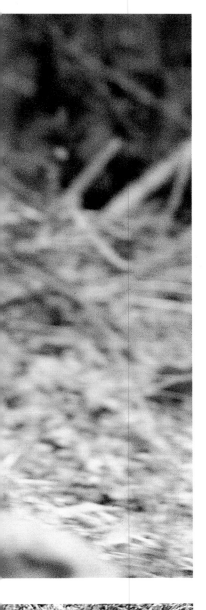

ABOVE LEFT: The adult males often try to intimidate others by showing off their strength and size in noisy displays during which they charge, throw stones, drag branches and shake small trees. These displays minimise the need to establish dominance through fights, although fights do also occur.

ABOVE: Chimpanzees, if given the opportunity, will steal and eat human babies. As a child this man saved his baby brother from chimpanzees but was mutilated himself before his parents managed to reach the scene and save him.

LEFT: I have known this adult male chimpanzee since he was born and he is completely habituated to my presence. Adult males are about four times as strong as an adult man and have enormous canine teeth, but these wild chimpanzees did not realise this.

OVERLEAF: Now old enough to defend himself, my son has become good friends with the Tanzanian, Mwalidi, who was originally employed to act as his bodyguard when his mother and I were working in the forest, and they often explore Lake Tanganyika together.

but also numerous plant species. Ultimately this spells disaster for man. We depend on wild plants to provide us with food and medicines; and may well end up destroying ourselves. Many people believe that we can provide these things through the plants we cultivate and artificial substances produced in laboratories. The following two examples will show that this is not always so.

In the 1960s literally two grains of rice probably saved millions of people from starving. At the time a virus to which there was no known resistance was affecting world rice production. The International Rice Research Institute investigated about ten thousand varieties of rice, hoping to find a resistant gene. They finally examined one hundred seeds of a wild rice variety which they had in their collection. In two of those seeds they found a resistant gene. So they went back into the wild to collect more specimens with the gene. None was found. So they used the two existing grains to develop a resistance to the virus and now every modern rice plant has a gene which originated from those two vital seeds. And they certainly turned out to be absolutely vital because no other resistance to that particular virus has ever been found.

Throughout history malaria has killed millions, if not tens of millions of people. The first effective cure for malaria came from the South American cinchona tree whose bark produced quinine. Synthetic malaria cures are still based on the structure of natural quinine. These synthetic cures are cheaper to produce and in some cases more potent than natural quinine. However, malaria parasites are adept at becoming resistant to all known quinine substitutes and recently a deadly strain of malaria evolved in East Africa and started to spread. Again the lives of millions of people were at risk. Luckily, the malaria parasites have not yet managed to develop a resistance to the natural quinine extracted from the bark of the cinchona trees.

About 7000 medical compounds have been extracted from plants so far. As we know new diseases can suddenly appear among humans. It is quite possible that a plant which could treat a new disease has already been exterminated.

Apart from needing plants for food and medical sources, people will increasingly need wild places to find occasional peace from the traumas of city life. When I visit developed countries and especially large cities it always strikes me that the inhabitants live under tremendous pressures. These are not only due to limited space and the competition for jobs, but also to the flow of bad news engulfing everyone through radio, television and the daily papers. It seems to be making large sections of the population depressed and this may, as is normal with depression, result in an inability to see or create things of beauty.

The wildlife photographer has a responsibility to help people be fascinated by life and to show them some of the beautiful things which still exist so that those who are not fortunate enough to experience such things personally can at least see them through the photographer's eyes and, more importantly, through his heart and soul.

Acknowledgments

I should like to express my gratitude to the many people who have helped me in my work amongst the wild animals in Africa. Numerous Tanzanian government officials, including those of the Tanzanian National Parks and of the Ngorongoro Crater Authority, invariably encouraged me in my attempts to portray the behaviour of the animals and the splendour of their country.

My thanks are also due to a great number of acquaintances and friends who, through many years and in a variety of ways, both in Africa and elsewhere, helped to make my work possible. I should specifically like to mention Jane Goodall, Louis and Mary Leakey, John Owen, Myles Turner, Sandy Fields, David Babu, Solomon Ole Saibull, Mr. Mgina, Kazim Nathani, George and Michael Dove, Chimenbhai and Jandu Patel, James Malcolm, Michael and Gisela Leach, Bert and Stephanie Von Mutius, Guy Parsons, Maggie Parker, John Goodrich, Lisa Halika, Aadje Geertsema, Ferry and Stella Kleemann, Tom Arnold, Dillie Keane, Robert and Helene Beck, Vincent Carroll, Joan and Arnold Travis, Hugh and Tita Caldwell, Ann Chegwidden, Bill and Virginia Travers, Joanne Hess, Dennis Kane, Mary Smith, David O'Dell, Ronald Altemus, Olivia Fackelmayer, Michael Rosenberg, Revel Fox, Dave Dickie, Victor Nunes, Christine Frederick, Toni Brescia, Diana Saltoon, Panya Bockelmann, Peter Marler, Maurice and Lois Marrow, Theresa Rice.

I should especially like to thank Karen Ross, who cheerfully tackled the library research on the prehistoric animals mentioned in this book. Conclusions drawn from fossil finds sometimes varied between different scientists and I chose the one which I found most convincing. In addition I added some theories of my own. Should any prove to be inaccurate then the responsibility lies with me.

I should also like to thank my Tanzanian assistants, Sirili, Renatus, Lawrence, Maro and Paulo, who have been the most marvellous and loyal companions throughout the many years of living in the wild in Africa.

I also owe much to my son, Hugo, who has been a wonderful companion whenever he joined me and on numerous occasions has shown great courage when faced with danger.

Index